Handbook of COBOL Techniques

Written by:
Computer Partners, Inc.

QED® Information Sciences, Inc.,
Wellesley, Massachusetts 02181

Published by
QED® Information Sciences, Inc.
QED Plaza, 170 Linden Street
Wellesley, MA 02181
Printed in the United States of America

First edition: December 1979
First revised edition: February 1982
Second printing: May 1982

© 1979 by QED® Information Sciences, Inc.,
and Computer Partners, Inc.
All Rights Reserved
Library of Congress Catalog Card Number: 79-67202
ISBN 0 89435-037-4

CONTENTS

PREFACE

Computer Partners, Inc. is a data processing consulting firm with offices in Boston and Chicago. The company provides education, consulting, systems design and implementation services to business and industry with specialization in the implementation of business applications software in data base and data communications environments.

A basic philosophy of Computer Partners is to deliver software products which are consistent in format and are readable, efficient and maintainable. In an attempt to insure that these objectives are met, Computer Partners developed a set of internal program development standards to guide its staff in the implementation effort and to provide a basis for product evaluation. During the past three years, these guidelines have been refined through constant use and additional experience, and have gained a high degree of client acceptability. Although originally conceived of as an internal document, clients have continually expressed a desire for copies of the guidelines for use by their own staff. It was the realization that these guidelines would be beneficial to most data processing installations that prompted the publication of this book.

The principle contributors in the development of this book were staff members with substantial exposure in systems implementation. Jeanne Bogart, Jeff Walker and Bill Heys deserve acknowledgement for the major effort.

I.
OBJECTIVES

OBJECTIVES

The COBOL programming language gives us the ability
to produce code which is more understandable and, therefore, more easily maintained. We sacrifice some efficiency
to reduce development time for initially writing and later
modifying our program products.

COBOL will not inherently guarantee programs that are
reasonably clear, efficient, or executable. As with any
language (including English), the users skill will determine
whether the result is extravagantly eloquent, unintelligible
or (as we hope) clear and succinct.

The objective of this book is to provide the programmer with recommendations and guidelines toward the goals
of consistent, easily understandable, and maintainable
programs. We should also strive for maximum efficiency
when it does not excessively compromise these objectives.

Many of our recommendations for COBOL formatting and
efficiency apply to IBM computers in the 370 and 3030
series or machines which are compatible with these IBM
computers. These computers use a hexidecimal bit configuration; therefore, arithmetic can be performed in
either packed decimal or binary. Computers which utilize
an octal bit configuration would, of course, be excluded
from any of the packed decimal considerations.

Many of our programming techniques may result in
slightly less efficient coding where the simplification
of the program makes it feasible to sacrifice some
computer efficiency for reduced development cost and
program maintenance. Most of our recommendations, however, will apply to any vendor's computer, from large main
frames to minis on which the COBOL compiler is available.
If your needs are for optimally efficient programs, you
may wish to alter some of our recommendations appropri-
ately.

II.
IDENTIFICATION
DIVISION

IDENTIFICATION DIVISION

The identification division serves as important documentation for the program. While not all the statements discussed below may be required or allowed by your compiler, these statements or similar comments should always be provided.

A.   PROGRAM-ID

Enter the program name used in the source and core image libraries.

B.   AUTHOR

Enter your name on the first line and your department or group on the second.

C.   INSTALLATION

Enter the company name and the division, subsidiary, or user group for whom the program is being written.

D.   DATE-WRITTEN

This should contain the date on which the coding of the program commenced.

E.   DATE-COMPILED

This will cause the compiler to supply the date on which the compile was run.

F.   REMARKS

The remarks section of the program should contain the program name plus a brief description of all major functions in the program. It is also helpful to provide a one line description of all program input and output. This is especially important for programs which access data bases, since most data management files do not appear in programs as SELECT, FD, and OPEN statements. It is, therefore, more difficult to quickly ascertain from the program the data files being accessed unless remarks are included.

Modifications, after the program has been accepted into production, should also be described in this section (programmer, date, and description of change). This provides a history of the program's evolution and documents the effective date of modifications.

REMARKS.
   ACCOUNT/PROJECT VERIFICATION PROGRAM

   PROGRAM READS SORTED ACCOUNT TRANSACTIONS AND VERIFIES THE
   ACCOUNT AND PROJECT NUMBERS.
   * VALID TRANSACTIONS ARE WRITTEN TO THE OUTPUT TRANSACTION FILE.
   * INVALID TRANSACTIONS ARE WRITTEN TO THE ERROR REPORT.
   * THE MASTER FILE IS UPDATED WITH THE VALID ACCOUNT/PROJECT
     NUMBERS.

   INPUT - ACCOUNT TXN FILE
           ACCOUNT MASTER FILE
   OUTPUT - VALID ACCOUNT TXN FILE
            UPDATE MASTER FILE
            ACCOUNT TXN ERROR REPORT
   -REVISIONS-
   DATE   WHO   DESCRIPTION

   8/2/79   T.GLICH   EXPANDED SIZE OF PROJECT NO. TO INCLUDE
                          A SITE CODE.

III.
ENVIRONMENT
DIVISION

ENVIRONMENT DIVISION

A.   Source and object computer entries should be supplied since it may allow the compiler to use an extended instruction set.

B.   SELECT statements should be listed in the same sequence as the FD's in the data division. The files are then presented in an organized manner to improve the clarity of the program.

C.   Use, as the file name in the SELECT statement, a descriptive name followed by "-FILE".

```
    SELECT  INVOICE-MASTER-FILE  ASSIGN TO  UT-S-INMASTER.
```

You may wish to use the technique of providing an 8-byte name (maximum) followed by "-FILE". This 8-byte name would be the name used as the DD name in the IBM OS/VS job control language.

```
    SELECT  ARMASTER-FILE  ASSIGN TO  UT-S-ARMASTER.

    //ARMASTER DD DSN=
```

D.   With IBM DOS, you should always choose the option of placing the file name at the end of the SELECT statement. This name will then be used in the job control DLBL statement. This facilitates the changing of physical device assignment.

```
    SELECT  ARMASTER-FILE  ASSIGN TO  SYS029-UT-3330-S-ARMASTER.

    // DLBL ARMASTER
    // EXTENT
```

E.   Some compilers and operating systems allow a choice between assigning a file to either a specific device or a mnemonic. If the choice is available, assign the file to a mnemonic. The program is then more flexible, and specific device assignment may be made at execution time.

F.   Some versions of COBOL provide for SELECT statements with many subordinate clauses (e.g. defining data bases). In this case, make the statement more readable by coding each subordinate clause on a separate line and indenting these comments.

```
SELECT SAMPLE-FILE
   ASSIGN INDEX TO
    FILEIX1
    VOLUME SIZE 40000
         CONTIGUOUS NO INITIALIZATION
    FILEIX2
   ASSIGN DATA TO
     FILEDB1
         VOLUME SIZE 50000
         CONTIGUOUS NO INITIALIZATION
     FILEDB2
   RESERVE 5 INDEX AREAS
   RESERVE 3 DATA AREAS
   ORGANIZATION IS INDEXED
   ACCESS MODE IS DYNAMIC
   RECORD KEYS ARE
      LEVEL1-KEY
      LEVEL2-KEY
      LEVEL3-KEY
   FILE STATUS IS COBOL-STAT
   INFOS STATUS IS INFOS-STAT
   ALLOW SUB-INDEX
   LEVELS ARE 3.
```

IV.
DATA
DIVISION

DATA DIVISION

A.   FILE SECTION

1. FD's should be sequenced in the program so that most frequently accessed files are coded first. For IBM compilers, permanent base registers will be assigned to the first five FD's in the program. When all five permanent registers have been assigned, temporary registers are used for any additional files.

2. The following format of FD's is suggested:

   a. Preceding each FD should be a couple of comment lines briefly describing the file.

   b. The FD and the file name should appear on one line.

   c. Following the FD should be a single line for each of the applicable clauses (e.g. RECORD CONTAINS, BLOCK CONTAINS, etc.) with each on a separate line and each starting in the same card column.

   d. The file record name should be an 01 level containing a picture which defines the length of the entire record. The data name used for the record should be the same name used for the file except that "-FILE' is replaced by "-REC'.

```
FD  EMPLOYEE-FILE
    BLOCK CONTAINS 0 RECORDS
    RECORD CONTAINS 90 CHARACTERS
    LABEL RECORDS ARE STANDARD
    DATA RECORD IS EMPLOYEE-REC.
01  EMPLOYEE-REC          PIC X(90).
```

3. Fields within records should not be defined in the file section. Record contents should be described in working storage, and READ INTO and WRITE FROM should be used to access records.

   There are two major reasons for this procedure. First, it is easier for the average IBM core dump reader to find the record when it is in working storage. Second, the records become unavailable after the write (also before the open and after the close) when data names are referenced in the FD. Someone may be maintaining your program someday and assume that data is available even after records are written.

A deviation from this technique regarding record description may be acceptable in the case of print output records. One may wish to define two subordinate 05 levels, a control character and a 132 position print line, within the FD record description.

4. On machines where efficiency is a prime consideration, working in the buffer may be dictated. Also, where core limitations require judicious use of working storage, the READ INTO/WRITE FROM technique may not be practical.

5. Use the BLOCK CONTAINS 0 RECORDS with OS/VS. This allows the blocking factors to be overriden by the job control language. Remember, if the BLOCK CONTAINS clause is omitted, the default is "1" and the job control language cannot override.

6. Specifying RECORD CONTAINS nn CHARACTERS causes the compiler to produce a warning diagnostic if the length does not agree with the picture in the record clause. It is also easier for others to determine the record length.

B.   WORKING STORAGE SECTION

The proper organization of data in the working storage section of a program will result in a program which is more efficient and easy to read, as well as being more maintainable. Items of similar characteristics or purpose (i.e. switches, counters) should be placed in adjacent areas. Use comments liberally to document these groupings of data. Make working storage visually attractive by aligning levels, clauses, data names, and so forth. Further, try to be consistent from one program to the next, particularly when developing new systems. An example would be organizing working storage similarly in all report programs in a system.

On most computers, particularly those using virtual memory, it will be more efficient if the data with high activity is placed at the beginning or in adjacent areas of the working storage section. This reduces the probability of paging since the more frequently accessed data will be contained in the same virtual page, and the high activity pages are retained in real memory. This efficiency consideration should not be used at the detriment of building a program that is understandable and readable.

An additional consideration in the structuring of working storage is the grouping of data items used in a common sub-routine or sub-function. This greatly simplifies the passing of data to lower level modules. This functional combining of data elements becomes particularly important in a structured programming environment. There are also efficiency ramifications since the data items used in a lower level routine are then more likely to be maintained in the same virtual page of memory.

1. General Data Description Rules

COMP (Binary) -
is recommended for items used as subscripts or for items used in extensive arithmetic. The compiler may be found to convert external numeric data to COMP since it results in more efficient arithmetic.

You should sign all COMP fields. Otherwise, an additional instruction will be generated to remove the sign whenever the value is changed. COMP items will be most efficient when restricted to less than five digits since halfword fields are generated.

COMP-3 (Packed Decimal) -
is the suggested numeric usage for all other numeric data fields (except for COMP as described above) which are used in comparison or arithmetic operations. COMP-3 fields require only half (approximately) the core and external storage space, and the compiler must convert external numeric data to COMP-3 for comparison or arithmetic operations.

You should sign all packed decimal fields. In addition, COMP-3 items should be defined as an odd number of digits. Otherwise, an extra instruction will be generated whenever the value is modified (to insert a zero in the odd position).

Alphanumeric -
is preferred for all other data items unless numeric display is absolutely necessary. PICTURE 9 requires additional instructions in moves, compares, and arithmetic operations and is more prone to data exception errors.

2. Levels

It is suggested that data items be grouped under 01 levels with other data items which have common characteristics (i.e. all switches) or other data items used in common functions. Two to four character prefixes should be used in each group to facilitate finding them in working storage and identifying their function in the procedure division. Suggested prefixes are discussed below under Data Names.

77 -
The use of 77 levels should be avoided for the reasons just stated. One, however, may be used at the beginning of the working storage section.

```
WORKING-STORAGE SECTION.

77  WS-ID                        PIC X(36)         VALUE
              'CPI0001 WORKING STORAGE STARTS HERE'.
```

The purpose of this literal is to simplify the process of locating working storage in an IBM core dump.

Ø1, Ø5, etc. -
Each successive sub-level of data, under a group, should be increased by 5 and indented. This simplifies the process of adding intermediary levels at a later time.

```
01  CALENDAR-REC.
    05  CAL-FIELD.
        10  CAL-MONTH    PIC X(02).
        10  CAL-DAY      PIC X(02).
        10  CAL-YEAR     PIC X(02).
```

88 - Levels
Used whenever practical to associate meaningful names with the value of an element. They should be indented from the associated elements' level number.

```
10  CAL-MONTH    PIC X(02).
    88  CAL-JANUARY      VALUE '01'.
    88  CAL-FEBRUARY     VALUE '02'.
    ETC.
```

3. PICTURE

The PICTURE clause may be abbreviated PIC and should start in the same column throughout the program. This greatly enhances the visual presentation of the program. The indenting of level numbers may occasionally cause the PIC clause to be placed on a line separate from the associated data name, but this is a small price to pay for a neatly organized working storage.

4. Data Names

The following guidelines are recommended for the assignment of data names:

a. Keep them as descriptive as possible while remaining reasonably brief.

b. Use a 2 to 4 character prefix for all data names.

c. Hyphenate for readability (e.g. AR-DATE-CLOSE not ARDATECLS).

d. Indicate key fields (e.g. ORD-K-NUMBER rather than ORD-NUMBER).

e. Standardize the data name for the same fields in different files by varying the prefix and retaining the suffix (e.g. record area ORD-PARTNO; print area PRT-PARTNO).

f. Do not use identical names with a qualifier. It is preferable to use the same name with different prefixes.

   INV-ACCT-NO instead of ACCT-NO OF INV-RECORD
   CUS-ACCT-NO instead of ACCT-NO OF CUS-RECORD

   Some data dictionary systems, however, will not allow the assigning of a variable prefix, based on elements use in several files. In this case, qualification may be necessary.

   The following prefixes are suggested.

   CNT   Counters

   HDG   Report heading lines (HDG1, HDG2, HDG3, etc. for multiple heading lines)

   PRT   Print detail lines (PRT1, PRT2, PRT3, etc. for details)

   TBL   Tables (arrays)

```
SUB   Subscripts

NDX   Indexes

BIN   Miscellaneous binary fields

DEC   Miscellaneous packed decimal fields

NUM   Miscellaneous Numeric Display fields

AN    Miscellaneous Alphanumeric fields

SW    Switches

LIT   Literals
```

Records should be assigned a 2 to 4 character prefix and all elements within the records should use the same prefix. The implementation of this technique is easy when using a source library for containing record descriptions.

```
CUS   for Customer file
ORD   for Order file
ITM   for Item file
INV   for Inventory file
AR    for Accounts Receivable file
EMP   for Employee file
SLS   for Sales file
PYL   for Payroll file
```

5. Accumulators

All accumulators should be packed decimal (if COMP-3 is available) unless they are used as indices, subscripts, or variable length record sizes. Binary arithmetic is more efficient for extensive computation or on computers without the packed decimal capability.

Accumulators should be grouped under a single 01 level with subordinate 05 levels to define sub-grouping such as:

a. Accumulators which are cleared together (total routines). These can be cleared with a group move instruction using a mask (see the Group Moves section of Efficiency Techniques.

b. Categories such as file counts, record counts, transaction counts, etc.

6. Program Logic Switches

The use of on/off switches to control the logic of a program should be restricted. An excessive number of switches makes the program very difficult to follow and is usually a result of inadequate thought during the logic development of the program. Often, you can test the data currently being processed for a particular condition instead of using a switch.

a. Establish all switches under a single 01 level in the working storage section. Individual switches should be 05 levels.

b. Each switch should be a single byte with a PICTURE X. This is preferable to PICTURE 9 if the element is not used arithmetically (see General Data Description Rules).

c. Zero should represent the "off" condition and one should represent the "on" condition. Level 88 conditional expressions should be established for each switch and should be used for testing the switch's setting.

d. Two techniques are suggested for naming 88 levels. One is to use descriptive names which read as English in an IF statement.

```
01  SWITCHES.
    05  SW-INPUT              PIC X(01)  VALUE '0'.
        88  SW-INPUT-PROCESSED           VALUE '1'.
        88  SW-LIGHT-NOT-PROCESSED       VALUE '1'.
```

If the above technique is used, it is very important to differentiate between the positive and negative conditions by including the word "NOT" or "NO" in the negative condition. Another technique is to use the switch name followed by "-ON" or "-OFF".

```
01  SWITCHES.
    05  SW-LIGHT           PIC X(01)  VALUE '0'.
        88  SW-LIGHT-ON               VALUE '1'.
        88  SW-LIGHT-OFF              VALUE '1'.
```

18

e. All switches should be initialized to the "off" condition. (Some compilers may automatically accomplish this.)

> *Use of excess logic switches*
> *Has caused untold program glitches.*
> *You clear and reset them,*
> *But, just once, forget them*
> *And switches can really be bitches.*

7. VALUE

Assigning an initial value to elementary data names in working storage is desirable; otherwise, these fields may contain garbage. Some compilers are self-initializing, but even then it does no harm to initiate a value. The program may someday be converted to run on other hardware which may differ in self-initializing characteristics.

The VALUE clause should be coded in the same column throughout the program, so they are aligned and easy to read.

8. REDEFINES

The REDEFINES is typically used for the following conditions.

a. To allow the same computer storage area to contain different data items or provide a method for giving an alternate description of the same data.

b. Tables; initializing of values.

c. Truncation or segregation of sections of a field.

d. Group levels for packing and unpacking when moving group level data to packed data or vice versa.

```
01  CAL-DATE.
    05  CAL-YEAR        PIC X(02).
    05  CAL-MONTH       PIC X(02).
    05  CAL-DAY         PIC X(02).
01  CAL-DATE-R  REDEFINES  CAL-DATE  PIC 9(06).
```

19

C.   LINKAGE SECTION

The linkage section of a COBOL program is misunder-
stood by many programmers. This section is not really in
your module at all; it is simply a means to allow you to
view or alter data which is part of a separately compiled
program module.

Your linkage section data names provide an ability to
reference data in a higher level module which dynamically
calls, or is link edited with, your program module. The
CALL which invokes your module passes one or more
addresses, each containing the starting point of data
which you are allowed to view. Your linkage section
entries provide a mask of data names which overlay areas
of memory beginning at the address(es) passed.

Because the data is part of a higher level program
module, there are certain explicit and implicit restric-
tions in the use of the linkage section:

a.   The VALUE clause is not allowed. The module
     which really defines the data (in working
     storage) is the one which may use the VALUE clause.

b.   The programmer must use care to insure that data
     is not modified which improperly affects the
     logic of the higher level module. If there is
     any doubt, perhaps the lower level module should
     store data values upon entry and restore prior
     to completion.

c.   Data which is passed to a subroutine should be
     placed contiguously in the working storage
     section of the higher level program. This
     simplifies the linkage between the modules by
     requiring fewer addresses to be passed.

V.
PROCEDURE
DIVISION

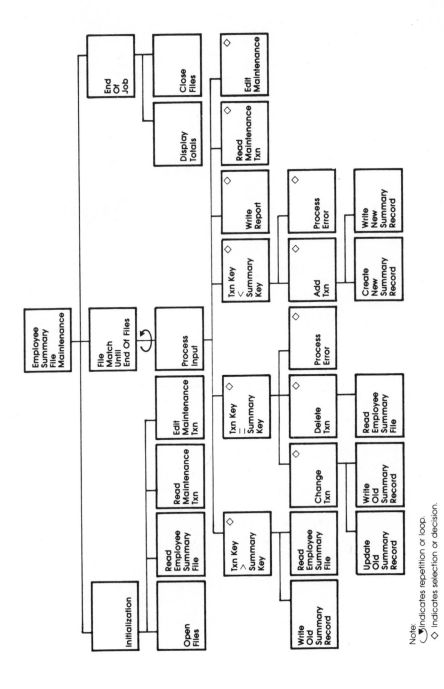

Note:
↻ Indicates repetition or loop.
◇ Indicates selection or decision.

22

PROCEDURE DIVISION

A.   LOGICAL ORGANIZATION

In order to create a consistent and professional
COBOL program, it is most important to establish techniques for the logical structure of the procedure
division. The use of a top-down structured approach is
recommended by the authors. The basic components of this
approach are outlined below.

1. Program Design

First a HIPO diagram, macro level flow chart, or
VTOC (Visual Table of Contents) should be created
for each program prior to beginning the actual
coding. This should contain, at a minimum, the logic
flow for the program mainline and major subroutines.
The development of this diagram is the initial step
in the design of a program. Our preference is a
VTOC (see sample) as it best represents the top-down
approach to program design.

This logic aid does not necessarily contain a
detailed, one for one, description of functions in
the program. It should instead document the logic
flow with only a brief description for each subroutine.

By reviewing this diagram, anyone maintaining the
program should be able to quickly determine the major
logic prior to looking into the COBOL coding.

2. The Driver

Each program should have at the beginning of the
procedure division no more than one page of code
which contains the initialization steps, a perform
statement which executes the main processing logic
until an "end-of-job" condition is met, and end-of-
job processing. This page of code is commonly
referred to as the "driver" or the "mainline".

The driver should be concise and ideally fit on
one printed page. Any major processing logic to
occur during program initialization or end-of-job
processing should be coded as separate subroutines.
When the initialization or end-of-job logic is
exceptionally concise, it is best to code these in-

line rather than as performed routines. The example
below is excerpted from the sample program.

```
0000-DRIVER.

*****          INITIALIZATION LOGIC

       OPEN INPUT EMPINSUM-FILE
                  MAINTCRD-FILE
            OUTPUT EMPOUTSM-FILE
                   REPTEMPS-FILE.
       PERFORM 3000-READ-EMPINSUM THRU 3099-EXIT.
       PERFORM 3400-READ-MAINTCRD THRU 3499-EXIT.
       PERFORM 4000-EDIT-MAINTCRD THRU 4099-EXIT
           UNTIL SW-EDIT-TRANS-VALID.
       MOVE CURRENT-DATE TO H1-DATE.

*****          DRIVER CONTROLS PROCESSING OF INPUT
*****          UNTIL END OF FILE IS REACHED ON BOTH FILES

       PERFORM 1000-PROCESS-INPUT THRU 1099-EXIT
           UNTIL KEY-EMPINSUM EQUAL TO HIGH-VALUES AND
                 KEY-MAINTCRD EQUAL TO HIGH-VALUES.

*****          END OF JOB LOGIC

       DISPLAY LIT-EMPINSUM  CNT-EMPINSUM.
       DISPLAY LIT-EMPOUTSM  CNT-EMPOUTSM.
       DISPLAY LIT-MAINT-ADD CNT-MAINT-ADD.
       DISPLAY LIT-MAINT-CHG CNT-MAINT-CHG.
       DISPLAY LIT-MAINT-DEL CNT-MAINT-DEL.
       DISPLAY LIT-MAINT-ERR CNT-MAINT-ERR.
       CLOSE EMPINSUM-FILE
             EMPOUTSM-FILE
             MAINTCRD-FILE
             REPTEMPS-FILE.
       GOBACK.
```

3. Main Processing Logic

     The next level down in logic development is the
main processing procedure which is performed until an
end-of-job condition is met. This code will execute
the major processing functions and will decide what
major subroutines are performed and when they are
performed. The example below is also from the sample
program.

```
*****        MAIN PROCESSING LOGIC - PERFORMS FILE MATCH

1000-PROCESS-INPUT.

    IF KEY-MAINTCRD GREATER THAN KEY-EMPINSUM
        PERFORM 3100-WRITE-EMPOUTSM THRU 3199-EXIT
        PERFORM 3000-READ-EMPINSUM  THRU 3099-EXIT
        GO TO 1099-EXIT.

*****        IF INPUT TRANSACTION MATCHES EMPLOYEE ON FILE,
*****        PROCESS CHANGE OR DELETE (ADD IS ERROR).

    IF KEY-MAINTCRD EQUAL TO KEY-EMPINSUM
        IF MAINT-TRANS-CHG
            PERFORM 2000-UPDATE-EMPLOYEE THRU 2099-EXIT
        ELSE
            IF MAINT-TRANS-DEL
                PERFORM 2100-DELETE-EMPLOYEE THRU 2199-EXIT
            ELSE
                MOVE ERR-MSG-01 TO PR1-ERR-MSG.

    IF KEY-MAINTCRD LESS THAN KEY-EMPINSUM
        IF MAINT-TRANS-ADD
            PERFORM 2300-ADD-EMPLOYEE THRU 2399-EXIT
        ELSE
            MOVE ERR-MSG-14 TO PR1-ERR-MSG.

*****        WRITE-REPORT LINE AND
*****        READ AND EDIT NEXT INPUT TRANSACTION

    PERFORM 3200-WRITE-A-LINE THRU 3299-EXIT.
    PERFORM 3400-READ-MAINTCRD THRU 3499-EXIT.
    PERFORM 4000-EDIT-MAINTCRD THRU 4099-EXIT
        UNTIL SW-EDIT-TRANS-VALID.

1099-EXIT.
    EXIT.
```

4. Subroutines

    Each module which must be executed within your
COBOL program presents three distinct alternatives.

    a. Performed Subroutines
        The instructions may be coded and compiled as
        part of your program. The PERFORM verb will
        then be used to execute this code.

    b. Included Subroutines
        These instructions are coded and compiled as
        a separate program. Your program, in order
        to execute this code, includes all such sub-
        routines when the link-edit of the main
        program is accomplished.

        This subroutine is executed via the CALL
        statement and all data areas common to the
        "CALLer" and the "CALLee" must be passed
        between the two (linkage section data names

in the CALLee, working storage in the
CALLer). If the data is passed through
several levels of subroutines, it will be
linkage section data in all but the higher
level module which originally defines the
data.

c. Dynamically Called Subroutines
These subroutines are coded and compiled as
separate programs. They are not link-edited
with your program. Instead the execution of
such a subroutine will branch to a module
that is shared with any other programs which
execute the same subroutine.

There are advantages and disadvantages to each
alternative. Listed below are the general criteria
for selecting one over the other. The rationale for
this selection is summarized under each.

5. Performed Subroutines

Used for functions which by their nature are
unique to this one program. If performed subroutines
are used for code which is common to several programs, redundant maintenance must be accomplished
when changes are instituted.

Advantages:

Performed routines are more efficient than called
modules.

All data names from the main program are available to the subroutine.

It is easier to read this program since one
compile listing has all functions.

It is easier to keep code in contiguous areas of
memory to increase efficiency of virtual paging.

Disadvantages:

A change to any subroutine requires recompilation
of the entire program.

It is somewhat more difficult to determine which
routines will be affected by a change to a data
field.

With the CALLed modules only that data which is passed to the subroutine is available and control of data usage is, therefore, enhanced.

It is easier for programmers to violate structured programming principles. A program module can branch to any other instruction in the same compile. With CALLed modules programs are forced to leave via the exit (GOBACK).

6. Included Subroutines

Used for functions which may be executed from several higher level programs.

Advantages:

Changes need only be recompiled into the subroutine and then relink-edited into all programs which CALL the subroutine.

It forces a structured approach to programming (data isolation and common module exit).

Disadvantages:

Generally, it is difficult to read or write a file which is not opened in the same module.

More pieces are required to "read" a complete program.

Maintenance and coordination of members in the core image library is difficult (i.e. which modules include which modules).

7. Dynamically Called Subroutines

Used for functions where it is advantageous to share the same module code between concurrently executing programs. Data or logic which is modified by one program is accessible in its altered form to other programs which use the same subroutine.

Advantages:

Changes need only be compiled into the module and are automatically effective for all higher level programs.

No other program may use the module until it is
released (GOBACK) by the program which has
control.

In determining which parts of your program should
be performed or called, you must use common sense
when evaluating the criteria presented above.

Small, unique, or insignificant routines should
be performed. We would not appreciate the chance to
maintain a program with more than 20-30 separately
link-edited subroutines unless the documentation
(VTOC or HIPO) was excellent.

B.   PHYSICAL ORGANIZATION

While we should use the basic concepts of structured
programming, our major goal is a workable program that is
concise, understandable, maintainable, and as efficient as
possible within these guidelines. In order to satisfy
these requirements, we must establish techniques for
physically organizing the code. Following are suggestions
for producing a neat, consistent, and professional program.

1.   Indentation

Proper alignment of data names and verbs within
your program will greatly enhance the readability of
the listing. It also results in a much more visually
pleasing document.

a.   When using a compiler which observes standard
A and B margin rules, statements should begin
in column 12 unless they are conditioned by
an IF. On some newer compilers, the A and B
margin rules are not used, but you should,
nevertheless, maintain the same column
throughout your program.

b.   When a single statement exceeds one line,
indent the successive line(s). Two or four
columns of indenting is recommended.

c.   IF's

All statements relating to an IF should be
indented.

When IF's are nested, each level and its conditional statements should be further indented.

The ELSE should be on a separate line and
aligned with its IF.

```
IF CUS-ACCT-NO IS NUMERIC
    MOVE CUS-ACCT-NO TO TBL-ACCT-NO (NDX-ACCT)
    IF CUS-PROJECT = SAVE-PROJECT
        NEXT SENTENCE
    ELSE
        MOVE CUS-PROJECT TO OUT-PROJECT
ELSE
    PERFORM 7500-ACCT-ERROR THRU 7599-EXIT.
```

2. AND/OR conditions should be coded on separate
lines and the condition tests aligned. Parentheses
should be used to eliminate ambiguity even where the
compiler assumes the proper AND/OR relationships.

```
IF ORD-PART-NO = CUS-PART-NO
   AND (ORD-TYPE = WS-PRIORITY
   OR ORD-STATUS = WS-OVERDUE)
```

If you wish to highlight the condition, you may
want to code it this way.

```
IF ORD-PART-NO = CUS-PART-NO
        AND
     (ORD-TYPE = WS-PRIORITY
        OR
      ORD-STATUS = WS-OVERDUE)
```

3. READ and WRITE Options

AT END, INVALID KEY, AFTER POSITIONING, and other
clauses associated with file processing should be
coded on a separate line and indented from the READ
or WRITE. You may wish to further indent lines
relating to the AT END statement.

```
READ MASTER-FILE INTO MASTER-REC
    AT END
        MOVE HIGH-VALUES TO MAS-KEY-FIELD.

WRITE MASTER-FILE FROM MASTER-REC
    INVALID KEY
        DISPLAY 'XXXXXXXX - EXTENTS EXHAUSTED'.

WRITE REPORT-REC FROM DETAIL-LINE
    AFTER POSITIONING CARRIAGE-CONTROL.
```

4. Spacing

If you make liberal use of page ejects and blank
lines in your program, you can greatly improve a
program's readability. This may be accomplished by

using the SKIP and EJECT statements with some compilers or by using blank lines and special control characters with others.

Page ejects are very effective in setting off program divisions and sections, large record areas, major routines, or any other major blocks of code. Blank lines can be used to separate 01 levels, subroutines, or even complicated IF statements. If your compiler accepts either blank lines or SKIP statements, you may find blank lines preferable since they do not leave gaps in your line numbering.

On several minis, inserting a page eject character in your code affects the way the editor is used. Caution should be used in this situation, but learning to use the editor in this manner is worth the price of more visually appealing code.

5. Punctuation

    a. Commas –
        Commas are unnecessary and are not recommended unless they are contained in REMARKS lines or comments. Commas may be easily keypunched as periods and cause errors and/ or logic problems. Instead, items typically separated by commas should be written on separate lines.

        Not Recommended:

        ```
        MOVE WS-STATUS TO INV-STATUS, CUS-STATUS, ORD-STATUS.
        ```

        Recommended:

        ```
        MOVE WS-STATUS TO INV-STATUS
                          CUS-STATUS
                          ORD-STATUS.
        ```

    b. Periods –
        Use periods to close out every COBOL statement (even when they are not required).

6. Comments

    Asterisk comments should be used rather than NOTE statements. When NOTE appears as the first verb in a paragraph, all statements in that paragraph are also considered notes.

The deletion of existing COBOL statements preceding
a NOTE could cause the entire paragraph to be dis-
regarded.

Comments should be used liberally and are suggested in the following cases:

a. Preceding every major subroutine.
    One or two lines of comment are usually
    adequate except for complex subroutines.

b. Within subroutines to explain unusual
    instructions.

         CALL's to external modules
         Complex IF's
         Calculations

c. Preceding Source Library entries for record
    layouts.
    Use comments within the record layout to
    describe acceptable values for fields,
    meaning of indicators, etc.

d. Preceding any maintenance changes, describing
    the extent of the change, reason for, person
    performing the change, and the date of the
    change.

e. Comments can be made to stand out by using
    blank lines before and after, or by enclosing
    the comments in rows of asterisks.

```
*******************************************************************
*****    PRECEDE THIS COMMENT WITH A LINE OF                    *
*****    ASTERISKS. ALSO FOLLOWING.                             *
*******************************************************************

              OR

*****
*****    PRECEDE THIS COMMENT WITH A BLANK LINE.
*****    ALSO FOLLOWING.
*****
```

f. The actual comment can begin in any column,
    but you should avoid beginning in the same
    column as procedure division statements so
    they are more noticeable. We suggest begin-
    ning the text in column 20.

7. Paragraph Names

   a. We recommend paragraph names which start with
      a 4 digit sequence number followed by a
      hyphen and a descriptive name (3500 ROUTINE).
      Further, we suggest that these numbers be
      coded in sequence throughout the procedure
      division. You should leave gaps in the
      numbering scheme for later insertion of
      additional paragraphs.

      The purpose of this paragraph naming conven-
      tion is to facilitate the maintenance of your
      program. With logical ascending numbered
      paragraph names, every paragraph which is
      performed is simple to locate. This tech-
      nique is particularly helpful in large
      programs.

      The following is a suggested scheme for
      numbering paragraphs:

0000-0999	Driver
1000-3999	Main Processing Logic
4000-7999	Subroutines
8000-8999	Error Subroutines
9000-9599	Initialization Subroutines
9600-9999	End-of-job Subroutines

   b. Paragraph names are best coded on a separate
      line with no COBOL instruction on the same
      line.

   c. Paragraph names should be descriptive without
      being excessive in length. Hyphenate for
      readability.

   d. Perform EXIT's need not be given descriptive
      paragraph names. It is unnecessary to use
      any further paragraph name than "9999-EXIT"
      since it should be clear to which routine
      the exit belongs. We suggest that the sub-
      routine performed, in most cases, start on an
      XX00 paragraph sequence and end with an XX99-
      EXIT.

   e. If you use SECTION names, they should corres-
      pond to the paragraph number sequencing
      conventions.

See the section on the PERFORM verb for other comments.

C. COBOL VERBS

Included are comments on the most commonly used COBOL verbs.

1. ACCEPT

   a. ACCEPT, from the card reader, should only be used for single card input such as date cards or control cards. Other card files are better defined as COBOL files (with SELECT's and FD's) and accessed with READ statements.

   The reason for this recommendation is that any file of significant size should have a SELECT and FD. This is both an efficiency consideration and a matter of philosophy. In this way, all files (card types, printouts, etc.) are immediately apparent at the beginning of the program in the SELECT statements. Also, ACCEPT is less efficient than READ.

   b. ACCEPT, from the console, is not recommended under OS. The console operator has too many responsibilities to consider keying in program data.

   c. Under DOS, the console is frequently used for entry of conditional data, dates, etc. Determine your installation's preference, however, before using the console for input.

   d. When data is to be ACCEPT'ed from the console, we suggest this procedure:

      -Accept the data
      -Verify the data
      -DISPLAY the entered data for the operator's verification before continuing. It is a good practice to display on both the console and the printer. The messages serve as documentation of the program processing options.

   See the paragraph describing the DISPLAY verb for an example of the above procedure.

On smaller computer systems (DOS, mini-computers, etc.), the ACCEPT (in conjunction with DISPLAY) is a valuable tool to use with user controlled or parameter driven programs. Removing fixed values from the program code and providing for these values to be entered via ACCEPT statements during program initialization can greatly increase the flexibility of the program.

2. ALTER

The use of the ALTER verb is not recommended. It makes programs extremely difficult to follow since you cannot tell where a GO TO went to.

3. CLOSE

   a. We suggest closing all files in a single statement when possible (see exceptions listed under the open statement) to preserve program simplicity and to increase program efficiency.

   b. Under DOS, tape files should be CLOSED WITH LOCK if the tape is to be rewound and unloaded after program execution. If you fail to CLOSE WITH LOCK you run the risk of another program using your output tape as a scratch tape.

4. DISPLAY

   a. Under OS/VS, displays to the console should be avoided. Due to the volume of displays occurring on the console, the operator may easily miss these messages.

   b. On most computers, DISPLAY's to the printer should be restricted to low volume messages. Otherwise, create a print file and use the WRITE statement. One major reason for this is that it is extremely difficult to format print lines with a DISPLAY. In addition, DISPLAY is more time-consuming than WRITE.

   DISPLAY's may be used very effectively to display the contents of input control cards or input parameters which drive the program. A quick glance at the control parameters will indicate how the program was executed.

c. DISPLAY's are also a valuable tool in the testing phase of any program. The contents of a file may be displayed before and after update logic. The DISPLAY or EXHIBIT may be coded as a programmer's version of the ready/ trace option of COBOL to aid in the debugging or verification of the program logic. DISPLAY and EXHIBIT are not recommended, however, if the computer has a good interactive COBOL debug facility.

Under DOS, console messages may be used to notify the operator of exception conditions or to display messages used in conjunction with the ACCEPT verb. All console display should also be sent to the printer since the console hardcopy output may not be accessible to Data Control or to the programmer.

d. All messages displayed should be established in working storage and should not be coded as literals in the procedure division. This way each message is more easily maintained and need not be coded twice when the message is displayed to both the console and the printer. Each message displayed should contain the program number so the operator knows exactly which program is requesting input.

```
WORKING-STORAGE SECTION.
01  CONTROL-DATA.
    05  CONTROL-CODE                PIC X(01)    VALUE 'N'.
    05  CONTROL-DATE                PIC X(08)    VALUE SPACES.
01  MESSAGE-DATE.
    05  MSG-1                       PIC X(40)    VALUE
        'PGM12345 ENTER MONTH END DATE (MM/DD/YY)'.
    05  MSG-2                       PIC X(27)    VALUE
        'PGM12345 MONTH END DATE IS'.
    05  MSG-3                       PIC X(47)    VALUE
        'PGM12345 ENTER Y TO CONTINUE, N TO REENTER DATE'.

PROCEDURE DIVISION.
0100-GET-DATE.
    DISPLAY MSG-1.
    DISPLAY MSG-1 UPON CONSOLE.
    ACCEPT CONTROL-DATE.
    (VERIFY DATE)
    DISPLAY MSG-2 CONTROL-DATE.
    DISPLAY MSG-2 CONTROL-DATE UPON CONSOLE.
    DISPLAY MSG-3.
    DISPLAY MSG-3 UPON CONSOLE.
    ACCEPT CONTROL-CODE.
    IF CONTROL-CODE = 'N'
        GO TO 0100-GET-DATE.
```

5. EXAMINE

A very time-consuming statement that should be avoided. If testing and replacing a one-character value in a fixed position, use IF-MOVE instead.

6. GO TO

   a. The diabolical GO TO has, in the opinion of true structured programmers, been the cause of a majority of the unmaintainable programs in existence. The GO TO conversely believes that the programmer is at fault. We agree with the latter.

      We haven't a mind to say no to
      the use of the infamous GO TO.
      Instead we suggest
      that the IF in its nest
      is what we're inclined to say whoa to.

   b. A well designed structured program will eliminate the need for most GO TO statements. Within a well structured program, the GO TO should be restricted to the following uses:

      - Forward only to paragraph names within the subroutine

      - Forward to the subroutine EXIT

      Loops within programs should be driven by PERFORM--UNTIL from outside the loop rather than use a GO TO to the top of the loop.

   c. GO TO---DEPENDING ON may be used in certain cases to provide a choice between multiple processing options (the CASE structure in structured programming). Each paragraph which is the object of the GO TO should be coded so as to have the last statement a GO TO to a common EXIT.

```
4100-EDIT-REC.
    GO TO 4110-EDIT-1
           4120-EDIT-2
           4130-EDIT-3
           4140-EDIT-4
           4150-EDIT-5
        DEPENDING ON EDIT-CODE.
    GO TO 4190-INVALID-CODE.
4110-EDIT-1.
    MOVE . . .
       . . . .
    GO TO 4199-EXIT.
4120-EDIT-2.
    MOVE . . .
       . . . .
    GO TO 4199-EXIT.
4130-EDIT-3.
    MOVE . . .
       . . . .
    GO TO 4199-EXIT.
. . . . . . . . . . . . . . . . . . . .
4190-INVALID-CODE.
    MOVE . . .
       . . .
    GO TO 4199-EXIT.
4199-EXIT.
    EXIT.
* ENDCASE
```

7. IF

    a. Unfortunately, the nesting of IF statements
        presents two problems. The maintenance pro-
        grammer finds them difficult to change and
        occasionally cannot understand then entirely.
        It is best to restrict nesting to one or two
        levels. Three level nested IF's should be
        avoided, and any nesting greater than three
        is not recommended by the authors.

        One way to avoid the excess nesting of IF's
        is to make use of the villainous "GO TO"
        statement. There is nothing "unstructured"
        about GO TO's when they are used to simply
        bypass sections of code and remain within the
        major subroutine being performed.

    b. Avoid the NOT condition test, especially in
        compound conditional statements. It is
        confusing if the NOT is used in conjunction
        with multiple AND's and OR's within an IF

statement.   Positive condition tests are much easier to understand.

c.   Use 88-level names whenever possible rather than comparing to data names or literals. IF SW-LIGHT-ON rather than IF SW-LIGHT EQUAL TO '1'.   This is discussed further under Use of Literals in the Efficiency Techniques Section.

d.   Always test for the most-likely-to-occur condition first, and the least-likely last, so that the unnecessary execution of IF statements may be bypassed.

```
IF INV-ITEM IS NUMERIC
        ADD INV-ITEM TO CUS-TOTAL-ITEMS
        GO TO 3350-INVOICE-EDITED.
IF INV-TOTAL = CONTROL-TOTAL
        MOVE INV-TOTAL TO OUT-INV-TOTAL
        GO TO 3350-INVOICE-EDITED.
        .
        .
        .
3350-INVOICE-EDITED.
```

e.   Use parentheses to clarify complex IF statements.

```
IF (POLICY-STATUS = WS-INACTIVE) OR
   (POLICY-TYPE = MAST-TYPE-3 AND
    POLICY-YEAR = MAST-YEAR)
```

f.   Attempt to organize data so that the IF compares fields of the same usage, size, and number of decimals to increase efficiency.

g.   The IF...ELSE combination can also be used to generate another version of the CASE structure.

```
4100-EDIT-REC.
    IF EDIT-CODE = 1
        PERFORM 4110-EDIT-1
    ELSE IF EDIT-CODE = 2
        PERFORM 4120-EDIT-2
    ELSE IF EDIT-CODE = 3
        PERFORM 4130-EDIT-3
    ELSE IF EDIT-CODE = 4
        PERFORM 4140-EDIT-4
    ELSE
        PERFORM 4150-EDIT-5.
* ENDCASE
```

8. MOVE

    a. Attempt to organize data so that MOVES occur
        between data names

            of the same usage,
            of the same length,
            of the same number of decimal places.

        COBOL will generate more efficient code.

    b. The use of MOVE CORRESPONDING is not recom-
        mended. This may cause problems if the data
        names in one of the structures are altered.
        It also results in a considerable amount of
        excess coding to qualify the data names when
        used in other instructions.

9. OPEN

    All files should be opened in a single statement
if possible. The machine will only have to link to
the open routines once (OPEN is extremely costly).
Align the INPUT, OUTPUT and file names for readability.

```
OPEN    INPUT     TXN-FILE
                  MASTER-FILE
        OUTPUT    NEW-MASTER-FILE
                  REPORT-FILE
```

    For consistency, we suggest that input files and
output files be opened in the same sequence as
listed in the FD's and SELECT's.

10. PERFORM

   a. All PERFORM's should be through an EXIT.
      While this may appear to cause excess coding,
      especially for small subroutines, we should
      assume that someone will be required to add
      a substantial amount of code to a subroutine
      and require a "GO TO" to the paragraph's
      exit. Section PERFORM's are not recommended
      but when used should also be through an
      EXIT.

   b. PERFORM's using the VARYING and UNTIL
      options are encouraged; they are more under-
      standable, more efficient, and less likely
      to result in program loops than simple
      performs where the incrementing of indexes
      and testing of exit conditions are coded
      within the subroutines.

   c. PERFORM's should be used when the subroutine
      is executed from more than one place in the
      program and when it is sufficiently large to
      make redundant coding infeasible. If the
      subroutine is repeated many times, main-
      tenance is more difficult and risky.

   d. Subroutines which are performed should be
      placed, when practical, in close proximity
      to the performing module.

   e. Each performed subroutine should be associ-
      ated with one and only one exit. It is
      suggested that you do not PERFORM through an
      exit other than the one associated with the
      PERFORM. Later program changes may alter the
      structure of the program.

      2000-CLEAR-1.
            .
            .
      2099-EXIT. EXIT.
      2100-CLEAR-2.
            .
            .
      2199-EXIT. EXIT.
      2200-CLEAR-3.
            .
            .
      2299-EXIT. EXIT.

Recommended:

```
PERFORM 2000-CLEAR-1  THRU 2099-EXIT.
PERFORM 2100-CLEAR-2  THRU 2199-EXIT.
PERFORM 2200-CLEAR-3  THRU 2299-EXIT.
```

Not Recommended:

```
PERFORM 2000-CLEAR-1  THRU 2299-EXIT.
```

11. READ and WRITE

a. Each file should have only one READ and/or
    WRITE statement. The READ or WRITE for each
    file should be contained in a performed sub-
    routine. This greatly facilitates changes
    (and they will occur) such as selectively
    bypassing records, reformating of data, and
    accumulating record input and output control
    totals.

    The printer file is an obvious exception to
    this rule and will usually require a single
    write for the detail line and separate writes
    for each heading or total line.

    Another exception is data base input/output
    which on some mini computers is performed with
    READ and WRITE instructions. The subordinate
    clauses required for these type of operations
    make the one-access-per-file technique
    impossible.

b. Each file should maintain a record count, and
    this count should be displayed as part of the
    end-of-job procedure.

c. Printer output should be produced on an inter-
    mediate disk file rather than directly to the
    hard-copy device. This occurs automatically
    on IBM OS/VS (SYSOUT data sets) and on IBM
    DOS using POWER.

    If there is no automatic capability to spool
    the printout to an intermediate disk (or
    tape) device in your environment, you should
    consider creating all print output on disk or
    tape and using a standard utility to perform
    the disk to printer operation. This utility

print should provide capabilities to inter-
rupt and restart, produce multiple copies,
and skip over pages.

When output is written directly to a printer,
we run the risk of lost output due to
printer jams, carriage type problems, lost
reports, etc. Printer output which is
spooled to an intermediate device provides
printer restart as well as giving operators
a greater ability to maximize the scheduling
of the printer device.

d. When deciding whether to use AFTER POSITION-
ING, AFTER ADVANCING, or any other option
available with your installation's compiler,
learn your printer's characteristics and
determine what is the most efficient option
for your printer.

12. ROUNDED

Use the rounded option of COBOL rather than adding five to the least significant digit. This will
prevent a rounding problem if the precision of the
data changes. Several costly instructions, however,
are required to perform rounding, so eliminate any
unnecessary use of the statement.

13. STRING

This requires a complex subroutine and is time-
consuming. A byte-by-byte MOVE loop is usually more
efficient. Use STRING cautiously.

14. TRANSFORM

This is another time-consuming verb. With items
of 12 or fewer characters, EXAMINE...REPLACING is
more efficient.

15. UNSTRING

Similar to STRING, this verb is costly and should
be used cautiously. It is better to redefine the
data as a table of one-byte fields and unstring it
with IF and MOVE statements.

D.   EFFICIENCY TECHNIQUES

The programmer's goal should be to write programs which can be processed most efficiently without sacrificing clarity or maintainability. We should not, therefore, write extremely complex routines when simple straightforward coding can accomplish the function, even at the expense of a few CPU cycles. Complex routines should be used only when the efficiency considerations are significant and, then, these routines should contain comments sufficient to make them understandable.

We will be discussing, for the most part, efficiency considerations which should have no effect on the program's clarity. They simply allow COBOL to generate more efficient code.

1. Arithmetic Operations

(IF, MOVE, COMPUTE, ADD, SUBTRACT, MULTIPLY, DIVIDE)

a. Packed decimal or binary (depending upon machine type) is preferable for fields which are edited to print lines. Numeric fields contained in file records should also be packed (or binary) since peripheral storage space and channel transfer time can be reduced.

Fields used as subscripts or as length attributes for variable length record should be stored as binary format. For numeric fields which may contain extremely large values, it might also be advantageous to store this data, both internally and on peripheral files, in binary format.

Binary arithmetic is actually more efficient and can save storage space for very large numbers. A 9 digit number can be held in 4 bytes COMP where COMP-3 would require 5 bytes. A 7 digit number is a trade-off, requiring 4 bytes for either method. The problems with binary numbers are that they are more difficult to interpret in core or file dumps and, when they are printed, they must first be converted (by COBOL) to packed format. Binary fields must, further, be aligned on half or full word boundaries.

b. For those fields which are logically numeric
    but are not used in any arithmetic opera-
    tions (e.g. WORK STATEMENT #), define them as
    character fields rather than as numeric.
    This practice will lessen the chance of data
    exceptions.

c. Use the COMPUTE verb for all calculations
    except simple ADD or SUBTRACT. COBOL will
    generate more efficient code by using its
    own work areas.

    In addition, use parentheses to eliminate
    ambiguity for multiple operations.

        COMPUTE A = B + (C * (D + E))

    Do this even when COBOL would have evaluated
    the statement correctly; it serves to better
    document the program to the maintenance pro-
    grammer. Parentheses are, of course, un-
    necessary when ADD's and SUBTRACT's or
    MULTIPLY's and DIVIDE's are not mixed.

d. If a field has never been edited prior to
    your program, test for zero in the divisor
    before DIVIDE. This will eliminate program
    checks due to decimal divide exceptions.

e. The use of "ON SIZE ERROR" should be elimi-
    nated by allowing a sufficient number of
    digits to prevent overflow. "ON SIZE ERROR"
    should not be used to trap division by zero
    as it is less efficient than coding the test
    yourself.

f. Sign all fields unless absolute values are
    required.

g. In reversing the sign of a field, it is more
    efficient to subtract from zero than multiply
    by minus 1.

        COMPUTE FIELD-XYZ = 0 - FIELD-XYZ.

2. Numeric Field Validations

    Only the program which initially accepts and
validates the data should perform the numeric check.
All subsequent programs using the field should
assume that numeric data is contained and should

not reverify the fields.

There will be occasions when your program bombs due to invalid data on file, however, the fault should be shifted to the program which created the data, and any fix made to your program should be temporary, until the file is corrected.

3. I/O Optimization - Blocking and Buffering

On IBM 360/370/3030 series machines, care should be taken in blocking files. High-volume sequential files should have fairly large blocks containing a number of logical records. This will have a major impact on CPU time as every READ or WRITE causes a new physical block to be read or written and thousands of instructions are subsequently generated. Additionally, specify two or more buffers on high-volume sequential files to allow physical I/O on the file to occur concurrent with program execution. Low-volume files, on the other hand, should have small blocks and single-buffering because the trade-off of additional overhead for small blocks may be offset by the saving of memory.

Blocking and buffering are determined by the storage device as well as by program use. The block size can have serious impact on the amount of usable space on disk. Therefore, if you are not suffi-ciently familiar with the hardware and software environment in your organization to enable you to make efficient decisions regarding the blocking of files, you should check the specific reference manuals or check with your support personnel before establishing the block size.

4. Condition Testing

In testing a field for one of several values, always attempt to test for the most likely condition first. Examples of this would be:

Program with many transaction types where 90% of the transactions are of a single type.

Status codes returned from a data base call.

Less than, greater than, equal to testing in a table lookup.

5. Group Moves

A group of related fields which must be repetitively initialized during the program should use group, rather than individual moves whenever possible. Examples of this would be initialization of record areas prior to processing add transactions or clearing of accumulators during program control breaks. A dummy group (mask) area can be established in working storage containing the initialized value; the dummy area can then be moved over the area to be initialized. This dummy area and its use should be well commented within the program since any change to the size or length of the area being initialized must be correspondingly made to the dummy area.

```
     WORKING-STORAGE SECTION.
****
****          CONTROL FIELDS FOR PROCESSING UPDATE TRANSACTIONS
****
     01  CONTROL-FIELDS.
         05  CNTL-CODE                  PIC X(01).
         05  CNTL-DATE                  PIC X(08).
         05  CNTL-COUNTERS.
             10  CNTL-COUNT1            PIC S9(5)     COMP-3.
             10  CNTL-COUNT2            PIC S9(5)     COMP-3.
             10  CNTL-COUNT3            PIC S9(5)     COMP-3.
         05  CNTL-TOTALS.
             10  CNTL-TOT-PRICE         PIC S9(5)V99 COMP-3.
             10  CNTL-TOT-DISC          PIC S9(3)V99 COMP-3.
             10  CNTL-TOT-AMT           PIC S9(7)V99 COMP-3.
****
****          MASK FOR RE-INITIALIZING CONTROL FIELDS
****          WHEN UPDATE STATUS CODE CHANGES
****
     01  CONTROL-MASK.
         05  FILLER                     PIC X(09)     VALUE SPACES.
         05  FILLER                     PIC S9(5)     COMP-3 VALUE +0.
         05  FILLER                     PIC S9(5)     COMP-3 VALUE +0.
         05  FILLER                     PIC S9(5)     COMP-3 VALUE +0.
         05  FILLER                     PIC S9(5)V99 COMP-3 VALUE +0.
         05  FILLER                     PIC S9(3)V99 COMP-3 VALUE +0.
         05  FILLER                     PIC S9(7)V99 COMP-3 VALUE +0.
     PROCEDURE DIVISION.
         .
         .
         .
     3200-NEW-STATUS-CODE.
         PERFORM 4500-PROCESS-CONTROLS THRU 4599-EXIT.
         MOVE CONTROL-MASK TO CONTROL-FIELDS.
         .
```

6. Temporary Files

Using a file over and over for temporary storage and performing OPEN-WRITE-CLOSE and OPEN-READ-CLOSE sequences many times should be avoided. OPEN and CLOSE statements are extremely costly. READ and WRITE are also far costlier than most verbs. A table is significantly more efficient and should be considered as an alternative where the maximum size is reasonable.

7. Use of Literals

The use of literal values in the procedure division of a program should be extremely limited. The primary reason is to reduce any hard-coded dependencies on literals (such as testing for a specific value). If the literal is defined as a value in working storage, the program is more easily maintained. Figurative constants, however, such as SPACES, ZEROES and the NUMERAL 1 (to increment or decrement indexes) are conditions where a literal is justifiably defined in the procedure division.

In all other cases, the value is better assigned in the working storage section or defined in an external control card or parameter file and established during program initialization.

An example of this would be in the establishment of a maximum number of entries in a table. This maximum number of entries should be coded as a value in working storage. This value corresponds to the OCCURS quantity for a table. In general, this maximum value will be referenced a number of times during the program (e.g. table loading, search, etc.). The table size can now be changed simply by changing the OCCURS clause and the VALUE for the maximum number of entries. The procedure division is unaffected.

It is suggested that the use of literals in the procedure division be restricted to those cases mentioned below. In all other cases, you should create data names, with values, in working storage and reference these names in the procedure division.

Conditions where literals are recommended:

a. Adding + 1 to counters

b. MOVE ALL "literal" to initialize large fields to a constant value

c. Setting indexes to, up by, or down by, 1

d. Unique literals which are referenced by only one statement in the program and which by their nature will never change.

The advantages to using literals are that they are somewhat simpler to code and they make the program easier to read since the value is right there and does not require a reference to working storage.

The disadvantage of literals occurs when they are referenced by many statements and maintenance requires a change to the value.

8. Parameter Driven Programs

The flexibility of the program can be greatly increased by removing fixed values from the working storage area of the program and providing for these values to be entered via control cards or parameter files during program initialization.

This technique should be considered for use whenever a value is used for computation or comparison and could be subject to change in the future. It will prevent program modifications and recompilations when these values change; the change can then be accomplished simply by reloading the parameter file record or changing the control card.

9. Use of the Sort Verb

Whether internal or external sorts are to be used should be determined by the type of computer you are using. Some of the newer mini-computers offer only an internal sort, so the decision is clear. On large IBM main frames, the external sort is preferable as changes to the sort sequence may be made without program recompilation.

Internal COBOL sorts should be used only in the following cases:

a. The sequence in which data is to be used or reported will by the very nature of the program never be changed.

b. Multiple input files are to be merged and re-formatted prior to the sort function. It may also occur where a single input file has different record types which require formatting of the sort key. In these cases, the internal sort eliminates the need for a separate program simply to merge and/or reformat data.

The major disadvantage of the internal COBOL sort is that the program must be recompiled to change the sort sequence. It is quite often advantageous, especially for report programs, to have the flexibility of changing the sequence of the input data.

It is also advantageous at times to have the flexibility to use the sorted file to run additional reports, and this cannot be accomplished if the sort is embedded.

The moral of the story is that internal sorts have their uses; however, they should not be used simply out of habit or because they make the job control language somewhat easier to generate. If you make a mistake in setting up an external sort control card, you can simply correct the control card and try the sort again; if an internal sort were used, you would have to correct the program, necessitating a recompile.

10. Table Processing

The following are suggestions when building and accessing tables:

a. Building Tables

    (1) Load the table in sequence, when possible, by sorting the input data and sequence-checking the data to insure validity.

    (2) If the table access volume is high and the table has a large number of entries, an unsequenced table is inefficient and prevents the use of SEARCH ALL. You should, then, consider a method of sequencing the table after loading if it cannot be externally sorted.

    (3) The table's maximum number of entries should be stored as a data name in working storage. The load routine should check to ensure that this is not exceeded as opposed to testing for a literal.

    (4) If a high percentage of access is against a small percentage of table entries, an unsequenced table, with the

popular entries at the top, will be more efficient.

(5) If the table is built throughout the program (as opposed to loading during initialization) and the data is not sequenced, the following options are available.

    (a) Leave the table unsequenced, but, if it is large and accessed frequently, it will be inefficient. If the data is for an end-of-job report, it will probably have to be sequenced anyway.

    (b) Preload the table with key values if they can be anticipated (e.g. if program must accumulate totals by state, the state tables can be prebuilt and subsequently updated).

    (c) Maintain the table in sequence by
      - inserting and pushing down.
      - maintaining an unsequenced table with a sequenced linkage chain within the members.

(6) Initialize the table key fields to high values or all nines at the time the program is compiled. Initialize data fields to spaces or nines depending on usage.

b. Accessing Tables

(1) Technique for table lookup - depending on size of table.

    (a) Tables with very few entries (less than 10) should be accessed using separate data names and separate IF statements if it is determined that there is very little likelihood the table will grow. If the number of entries may increase, it is better to set it up as an indexed table and process as such.

    (b) Tables containing up to 50 entries should be accessed using the SEARCH

verb. SEARCH begins at the first
table element and searches sequentially through the table.

Note: On most compilers, the value
of the index is not reset to 1
automatically by the SEARCH verb
and must be reset by the program if
you wish to start at the beginning
of the table each time.

(c) Tables in excess of 50 entries, in
sequence, should be accessed using
the SEARCH ALL verb. SEARCH ALL
performs a binary search by beginning at the midpoint of the table,
testing for high or low, and then
picking the midpoint of the remaining entries, testing for high or
low, etc.

(2) Limit all searches by storing the value
of the highest index used during the
table load and testing this value during
the search process. If the table is
sequenced, test the search key for
"greater than" the table key.

Example:

```
SEARCH TABLE  AT END GO TO 2000-NO-ENTRY
    WHEN SEARCH-KEY = TABLE-KEY (INDEX-1)
        GO TO 3000-PROCESS-TABLE-ENTRY
    WHEN SEARCH-KEY GREATER THAN TABLE-KEY (INDEX-1)
        OR INDEX-1 GREATER THAN MAX-INDEX-1
        GO TO 2000-NO-ENTRY
```

(3) If a table entry is used in more than
one place after being accessed, move it
to an unindexed data name rather than
repeatedly using the indexed data name.
COBOL will generate more efficient code.

For Example:

```
01  TX-TABLE.
    05 TX-ENTRIES   OCCURS 50 TIMES INDEXED BY IDX.
        10  TX-1    PIC X.
        10  TX-2    PIC 999.
        10  TX-3    PIC S9(7) COMP-3.
```

Instead of constantly using TX-1 (IDX)
and TX-3 (IDX) etc. move TX-Entries
(IDX) to a separate definition which is
not an indexed field and use it in
further logic routines.

```
01  TRANS.
    05 TRANS-1      PIC X.
    05 TRANS-2      PIC 999.
    05 TRANS-3      PIC S9(7) COMP-3.
```

c. Subscripting/Indexing

Indexing, rather than subscripting, should
normally be used for processing of tables.
Indexes are handled more efficiently since
they are resolved in address format at compilation time.

When Subscripting is used, the following
guidelines apply:

(1) All data names defined as subscripts
     should be contained under a single 01
     level group entry, and the usage should
     be binary.

(2) Separate subscripts should be established
     for each table. Sharing of subscripts
     for many tables is risky, especially in
     the maintenance of programs.

(3) All subscripts should be initialized to
     zero. Even though a compiler may be
     self-initializing it is better to set
     initial values. A computer conversion
     will then present fewer problems.

(4) For each table, a binary field should be
     established which contains the value
     corresponding to the maximum number of
     entries in the table.

(5) If a subscripted field is used often
     (without a change in the subscript
     value), move the data to a fixed loca-
     tion in working storage instead of
     repeatedly referencing the subscripted

data name. Otherwise, the generated code must repeatedly resolve the subscript.

(6) When looping through tables (building or accessing), check to determine that the table length is not exceeded by comparing the subscript value to a data name containing the maximum number of table entries.

This test for table overflow should be against a working storage data name and not against a literal coded in the procedure division. This greatly facilitates changes in table size.

Always pair the add instruction with a check for table-limit.

ADD +1 to SUB.

IF SUB GREATER THAN TABLE-LIMIT

It is also recommended that the limit check not be an "equal to". The equal condition may in some way be bypassed, and a loop may occur if the condition is never met.

Subscripting Example:

```
01  SUB-SCRIPTS                 COMP.
    05  SUB-ONE                 PIC S9(4)  VALUE +0000.
    05  SUB-TBL-MAX             PIC S9(4)  VALUE +0500.
01  TBL-TABLE.
    05  TBL-ENTRY               PIC XX     OCCURS 500 TIMES.


0100-READ-TABLE.
    ADD +1 TO SUB-ONE.
    IF SUB-ONE GREATER THAN SUB-TBL-MAX
        GO TO 0199-EXIT.
    MOVE TBL-ENTRY (SUB-ONE) TO PRINT-FIELD.
    GO TO 0100-READ-TABLE.
0199-EXIT.
    EXIT.
```

d. When Indexing is used, many of the guidelines established for subscripting are still applicable.

(1)   Separate indexes for each table are inherent to the indexing technique.

(2)   Indexes should be initialized to 1 by the SET instruction. (Indexes cannot be set to 0.)

(3)   For each table, a field should be defined to specify the maximum number of entries in the table. This field should be defined as binary.

(4)   If the indexed entry is to be used repeatedly, it should be moved to an un-indexed data element.

(5)   Looping through the table should still be controlled by checking the maximum limit field against the value of the index. Care should be exercised to prevent the index from exceeding the limit of the table.

(6)   Relative indexing may be helpful during processing:

      TBL-ENTRY (NDX + 3)

Indexing Example:

```
01  NDX-INDEXES.
    05  NDX-TABLE-MAX          PIC S9(4) COMP VALUE +0500.
01  TBL-TABLE.
    05  TBL-ENTRY              PIC XX    OCCURS 500 TIMES.
                                         INDEXED BY NDX-ONE.
    SET NDX-ONE TO 1.


0100-READ-TABLE.
    MOVE TBL-ENTRY (NDX-ONE) TO PRINT-FIELD.
    SET NDX-ONE UP BY 1.
    IF NDX-ONE IS GREATER THAN NDX-TABLE-MAX
        GO TO 0199-EXIT.
    GO TO 0100-READ-TABLE.
0199-EXIT.
    EXIT.
```

11. Special Registers

When requiring DATE, DAY, TIME, CURRENT-DATE, or TIME-OF-DAY, obtain the value once and store it in working storage. Special routines are needed every time these registers are referenced.

VI.
SUBROUTINE
LOGIC

PRINT ROUTINE LOGIC

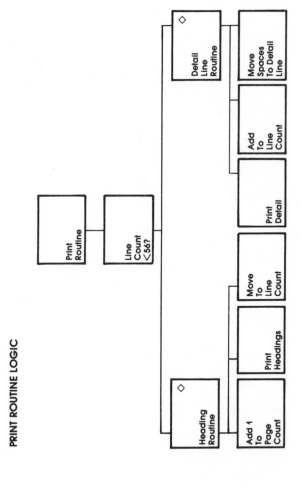

SUBROUTINE LOGIC

A.   PRINT ROUTINE

The following logic is suggested for print routines requiring page headings:

1.   Separate WRITE statements may be used for each heading line.

2.   If total lines are required, it is preferable to use the same WRITE instruction as the detail lines.

If this is not practical, the heading logic should be performed since it must be executed from two places (Detail Print and Total Line Print).

3.   The detail line should be filled prior to entering the print routine.

4.   Increment the line counter by the number of lines of paper used, not by the number of lines printed (e.g. If double spacing, add +2 and test for max lines; don't add +1 and test for half the max lines).

PRINT ROUTINE

```
0500-PRINT.
    IF CNT-LINE LESS THAN +56
        GO TO 0510-NO-HDG.
    ADD +1 TO CNT-PAGE.
    MOVE CNT-PAGE TO HDG-PAGE.
    WRITE PRINT-REC FROM HEADING-1
        AFTER POSITIONING TOP-OF-PAGE.
            .
            .
            .
            OTHER HEADING LINES
            .
            .
    MOVE ( THE # OF LINES USED BY THE HEADING ) TO CNT-LINE.
0510-NO-HDG.
    WRITE-PRINT-REC FROM DETAIL-LINE
        AFTER POSITIONING CONTROL-CHAR.
    IF CONTROL-CHAR EQUAL TO SINGLE-SPACE
        ADD +1 TO CNT-LINE
    ELSE
    IF CONTROL-CHAR EQUAL TO DOUBLE-SPACE
        ADD +2 TO CNT-LINE.
```

CONTROL BREAK LOGIC

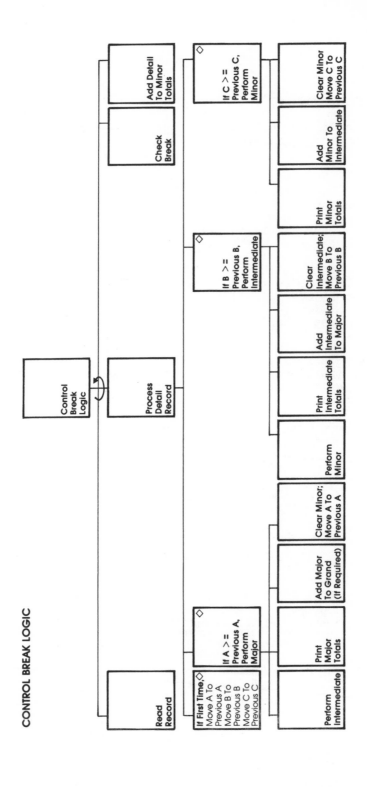

B.   CONTROL BREAK LOGIC

This logic will be used whenever a program is required to accumulate totals or perform special functions which summarize input detail at any number of levels.

The following assumptions are made:

The file must be in sequence by the control fields, major to minor.

All records come from one input file (if more than one were involved, the READ RECORD block would require a multifile merge).

The routine is flexible in that it is concise and easy to understand. Alterations to processing at any level (nonrepetitive code) and additions of new levels, if necessary, are easy to implement.

NOTES:

A = Major control fields.
B = Intermediate control fields.
C = Minor control fields.

Previous A, Previous B, Previous C = Hold areas for the previous records key.

FILE MERGE/SEQUENTIAL FILE MAINTENANCE

Note:
 ⟳ Indicates repetition or loop.
 ◇ Indicates selection or decision.

60

C. SEQUENTIAL FILE MAINTENANCE

The following logic is suggested for programs which must process add, delete, or change transactions against a sequential file.

It assumes that the new file must be created in its entirety; the file will not be updated in place.

It permits:

Add and change transactions to be entered in the same run. Add transactions must sort before the change transactions.

Delete and add transactions to be entered in the same run. Delete transactions must sort before the add transactions.

D. PROGRAM CONTROL TOTALS

Every program should maintain control counts of input files and output files. These control totals should be printed at end-of-job to verify that the program has run successfully. The counts may point out possible problems and will aid in problem solving.

```
READ MASTER-FILE INTO MASTER-RECORD
    AT END GO TO EOJ.
ADD +1 TO MASTER-RECORDS-IN.

WRITE MASTER-OUT FROM MASTER-RECORD.
ADD +1 TO MASTER-RECORDS-OUT.

IF TRANS-CODE EQUAL TO '1'
    ADD +1 TO ADDS-IN.
IF TRANS-CODE EQUAL TO '0'
    ADD +1 TO DELETES-IN.

DISPLAY 'XXXXXXXX - MASTER-RECORDS-IN  =' MASTER-RECORDS-IN.

DISPLAY 'XXXXXXXX - ADDS-IN            =' ADDS-IN.

DISPLAY 'XXXXXXXX - DELETES-IN         =' DELETES-IN.

DISPLAY 'XXXXXXXX - MASTER-RECORDS-OUT =' MASTER-RECORDS-OUT.
```

VII.
MISCELLANEOUS

MISCELLANEOUS

A. PLANNING AND TASK ESTIMATION

Prior to starting a program, you should create your own plan to complete the task. The following steps are suggested in this end:

1. Break down the program into smaller tasks.

*   Review of program requirements
*   Flow Chart, VTOC, HIPO
*   Coding
*   Desk Checking
*   Test Data Preparation (if required)
*   Job Control Language Preparation
*   Unit Testing
*   Documentation

2. Estimate the time required for each sub-task and establish target dates for their completion.

Review the relationships between tasks and schedule your activities to make optimum utilization of your time (e.g. don't wait until you've clean compiled to begin JCL and test data preparation).

In many cases, you will be working on several programs simultaneously, so each should be merged into your overall plan.

3. Maintain a record of actual versus estimated (elapsed time and man hours) to assist you in future estimating.

4. Check the availability of precoded source library file, record, and table definitions.

5. Check the availability and use of prewritten logic subroutines which will be included in the program.

        date conversions
        standard error routines
        standard access routines

B.   COMPILATION & TESTING CONSIDERATIONS

1.   Compiling

Compiles are time-consuming to execute and print. The following are some of the ways you can reduce this expense:

a.   Suppress cross-reference listings during testing. When the program is tested and ready to be released in production status, recompile the program including the sequenced cross-reference option. The maintenance programmer will be greatly aided by doing so.

b.   Desk check your source listing thoroughly to reduce the number of tests and recompilations. Play computer! Walk test data through the logic with pencil and paper.

c.   Desk check all changes thoroughly before submitting them for compiles.

Spelling of data names and paragraph names
Sequence numbers
Punctuation
Indenting

d.   Remove warning diagnostics where practical. It will be easier to spot important computer messages.

2.   Debugging

We all would, of course, prefer to write programs which are bug free. However, in the unlikely event that a program terminates abnormally during unit testing (probably due to the bad data, keypunch errors, or hardware malfunctions, not logic errors) the following guidelines should apply to the debugging of a program:

a.   Do not resubmit it immediately assuming that it was due to hardware, a power surge, operator error, or an act of God.

b.   Attempt to debug at the Source Code Level. Proper use of the STATE and FLOW COBOL options will prevent the need for most core

dumps. Use the COBOL interactive debugger
if one is available at the installation.

c. For initial testing with new JCL, avoid
getting core dumps because the most frequent
problems are caused by JCL errors before the
program even executes.

Core dumps should, in fact, be very infre-
quently required for debugging. Submit all
tests without the core dump option and rerun
the tests to obtain a dump only on those rare
occasions when the program cannot be debugged
at source level.

d. Protect against program loops. Under OS,
use a reasonable TIME parameter to soften
the pain of program loops. Under DOS,
inform the operator of the maximum elapsed
time your test should be allowed to run.

e. During initial tests consider the use of
strategically placed displays to:

Trace program logic
Display working storage fields
Display input or output records before
and after update logic

f. Get the most out of each compile. The ratio
of compile time to the actual execution of
the test is probably 10 or 20 to 1 on the
average. You should, therefore, attempt to
get the maximum out of each test.

The following are suggestions in this area:

Manipulate the output to obtain as many
results as possible before recompiling
to fix known problems.
During testing, allow the program to
continue even though the production
version might be terminated.

C. MAINTENANCE PROCEDURE

Once a program has been tested and turned over for
production, the following method should be used to document all subsequent changes to that program.

1. The program changes will be coded, compiled, and tested.

2. In a batch environment, all program update cards ought to be saved for a period of two weeks to provide for recovery of the source library. The latest update cards should be maintained in the card deck used to compile the program.

In a time sharing environment, it is advisable to keep program listings in each stage of development for a period of 2 weeks, depending upon the reliability of the installation. Keeping hard copy program listings is essential when modifying programs on-line. The powerful tool of time-sharing can be a nightmare when a program data set is accidentally deleted and the latest changes are not documented.

3. The programmer should write a brief description of the change (if not already provided by the user or the systems analyst) and document any extraordinary problems encountered in implementing the change. Also, a brief description of the change should be noted in the REMARKS section (as mentioned earlier in the IDENTIFICATION DIVISION section).

4. The computer printed sheet containing the source code changes should be attached to the description of the maintenance functions and filed with the program documentation. A brief description of the testing procedure might be included also.

5. If the change is other than a minor modification (e.g. 90% chance of success on first compile and test) then the following procedure might be considered when implementing the change:

a. Copy the source library member to another member name.

b. Make all changes to the new member name and also use that name to store the link-edited module in the core image library.

c. After all changes have been tested, rename the new source library member to the old member name after renaming the old member to a source name which can be purged.

d. Copy the new core image library member name
    over the old core image library member name.

e. In selecting new names for source and object
    members, be sure to use names which will be
    automatically reviewed for purging from the
    source and core image libraries.

VIII.
SAMPLE
PROGRAM

```
000100   ID DIVISION.                                                      CPI00001
000200   PROGRAM-ID.       CPI00001.                                       CPI00001
000300   AUTHOR.           COMPUTER PARTNERS, INC.                         CPI00001
000400                     34 WASHINGTON STREET                            CPI00001
000500   INSTALLATION.     WELLESLEY HILLS, MA. 02181                      CPI00001
000600                     COMPUTER PARTNERS, INC                          CPI00001
000700                     PERSONNEL DEPARTMENT                            CPI00001
000800   DATE-WRITTEN.     MARCH, 1979.                                    CPI00001
000900   DATE-COMPILED.    SEP 13,1979.                                    CPI00001
001100   REMARKS.          EMPLOYEE SUMMARY FILE MAINTENANCE.              CPI00001
001200                     THE PROGRAM READS MAINTENANCE TRANSACTIONS      CPI00001
001300                     AND UPDATES THE EMPLOYEE SUMMARY FILE.          CPI00001
001400                     TRANSACTIONS EITHER MAINTAIN OR DELETE          CPI00001
001500                     EXITING RECORDS OR ADD NEW RECORDS.             CPI00001
001600                     A REPORT OUTLINING THE MAINTENANCE IS           CPI00001
001700                     ALSO GENERATED.                                 CPI00001
001800   INPUT.            EMPLOYEE SUMMARY FILE  - EMPINSUM               CPI00001
001900                     EMLOYEE SUMMARY MAINTENANCE TRANSACTIONS  -     CPI00001
002000                     MAINTCRD                                        CPI00001
002100   OUTPUT.           UPDATED EMPLOYEE SUMMARY FILE  - EMPOUTSM       CPI00001
002300                     MAINTENANCE REPORT - REPTEMPS.                  CPI00001
002400                                                                     CPI00001
```

70

```
002600 ENVIRONMENT DIVISION.                                              CPIO0001

002800 CONFIGURATION SECTION.                                             CPIO0001

003000 SOURCE-COMPUTER.    IBM-370.                                       CPIO0001
003100 OBJECT-COMPUTER.    IBM-370.                                       CPIO0001

003300 INPUT-OUTPUT SECTION.                                              CPIO0001

003500 FILE-CONTROL.                                                      CPIO0001

003700******    INPUT EMPLOYEE SUMMARY FILE                              CPIO0001
003900    SELECT  EMPINSUM-FILE   ASSIGN TO UT-S-EMPINSUM.                CPIO0001

004100******    EMPLOYEE SUMMARY MAINTENANCE TRANSACTIONS                CPIO0001
004300    SELECT  MAINTCRD-FILE   ASSIGN TO UT-S-MAINTCRD.                CPIO0001

004500******    UPDATED EMPLOYEE SUMMARY FILE                            CPIO0001
004700    SELECT  EMPOUTSM-FILE   ASSIGN TO UT-S-EMPOUTSM.                CPIO0001

004900******    MAINTENANCE REPORT                                       CPIO0001
005100    SELECT  REPTEMPS-FILE   ASSIGN TO UT-S-REPTEMPS.                CPIO0001
```

71

```
005300 DATA DIVISION.                                                    CPI00001

005500 FILE SECTION.                                                     CPI00001

007700******          INPUT EMPLOYEE SUMMARY FILE                        CPI00001

005900 FD  EMPINSUM-FILE                                                 CPI00001
006000     BLOCK CONTAINS 0 RECORDS                                      CPI00001
006100     RECORD CONTAINS 40 CHARACTERS                                 CPI00001
006200     LABEL RECORDS ARE STANDARD                                    CPI00001
006300     DATA RECORD IS EMPINSUM-REC.                                  CPI00001
006400 01  EMPINSUM-REC                    PIC X(40).                     CPI00001

006600*****          EMPLOYEE SUMMARY MAINTENANCE TRANSACTIONS            CPI00001

006800 FD  MAINTCRD-FILE                                                 CPI00001
006900     BLOCK CONTAINS 0 RECORDS                                      CPI00001
007000     RECORD CONTAINS 80 CHARACTERS                                 CPI00001
007100     LABEL RECORDS ARE OMITTED                                     CPI00001
007200     DATA RECORD IS MAINTCRD-REC.                                  CPI00001
007300 01  MAINTCRD-REC                    PIC X(80).                     CPI00001

007500*****          UPDATED EMPLOYEE SUMMARY FILE                        CPI00001

007700 FD  EMPOUTSM-FILE                                                 CPI00001
007800     BLOCK CONTAINS 0 RECORDS                                      CPI00001
007900     RECORD CONTAINS 40 CHARACTERS                                 CPI00001
008000     LABEL RECORDS ARE STANDARD                                    CPI00001
008100     DATA RECORD IS EMPOUTSM-REC.                                  CPI00001
008200 01  EMPOUTSM-REC                    PIC X(40).                     CPI00001
```

72

```
008400******

008600 FD REPTEMPS-FILE
008700    BLOCK CONTAINS 0 RECORDS
008800    RECORD CONTAINS 133 CHARACTERS
008900    LABEL RECORDS ARE OMITTED
009000    DATA RECORD IS REPTEMPS-REC.
009100 01 REPTEMPS-REC.
009200 05 REPT-CTL-CHAR       PIC X.
009300 05 REPT-PRT-LINE       PIC X(132).
```

73

```
009500 WORKING-STORAGE SECTION.

009700 77  WS-ID              PIC X(36)             VALUE     CPI00001
009800                'CPI0001 WORKING STORAGE STARTS HERE'.   CPI00001
010000******                                                   CPI00001
          COUNTERS

010200 01  CNT-COUNTERS              USAGE IS COMP-3.          CPI00001
010300     05  CNT-EMPINSUM     PIC S9(5)     VALUE +0.        CPI00001
010400     05  CNT-EMPOUTSM     PIC S9(5)     VALUE +0.        CPI00001
010500     05  CNT-MAINT-ADD    PIC S9(5)     VALUE +0.        CPI00001
010600     05  CNT-MAINT-CHG    PIC S9(5)     VALUE +0.        CPI00001
010700     05  CNT-MAINT-DEL    PIC S9(5)     VALUE +0.        CPI00001
010800     05  CNT-MAINT-ERR    PIC S9(5)     VALUE +0.        CPI00001
010900     05  CNT-MAINT-CRD    PIC S9(5)     VALUE +0.        CPI00001
011100     05  CNT-LINES        PIC S9(5)     VALUE +99.       CPI00001
011200     05  CNT-PAGES        PIC S9(5)     VALUE +0.        CPI00001
011200     05  CNT-LINE-LIMIT   PIC S9(5)     VALUE +55.       CPI00001
011400******   ERROR MESSAGES                                  CPI00001

011600 01  ERR-MESSAGES.                                       CPI00001
011700     05  ERR-MSG-01           PIC X(35)  VALUE           CPI00001
011800          'ADD-EMPLOYEE IS ALREADY ON FILE'.             CPI00001
011900     05  ERR-MSG-02           PIC X(35)  VALUE           CPI00001
012000          'TRANS ID INVALID'.                            CPI00001
012100     05  ERR-MSG-03           PIC X(35)  VALUE           CPI00001
012200          'TRANS CODE INVALID'.                          CPI00001
012300     05  ERR-MSG-04           PIC X(35)  VALUE           CPI00001
012400          'STATE CODE INVALID'.                          CPI00001
012500     05  ERR-MSG-05           PIC X(35)  VALUE           CPI00001
012600          'DIVISION IS INVALID'.                         CPI00001
012700     05  ERR-MSG-06           PIC X(35)  VALUE           CPI00001
012800          'DEPARTMENT IS INVALID'.                       CPI00001
012900     05  ERR-MSG-07           PIC X(35)  VALUE           CPI00001
013100          'EMPLOYEE NUMBER IS INVALID'.                  CPI00001
013200     05  ERR-MSG-08           PIC X(35)  VALUE           CPI00001
013300          'EMPLOYEE NAME IS INVALID'.                    CPI00001
013400     05  ERR-MSG-09           PIC X(35)  VALUE           CPI00001
013500          'ANNUAL SALARY IS INVALID'.                    CPI00001
013600     05  ERR-MSG-10           PIC X(35)  VALUE           CPI00001
013700          'HIRE DATE IS INVALID'.                        CPI00001
013800     05  ERR-MSG-11           PIC X(35)  VALUE           CPI00001
013900          'EMPLOYEE HAS BEEN DELETED'.                   CPI00001
013900     05  ERR-MSG-12           PIC X(35)  VALUE           CPI00001
014000          'EMPLOYEE HAS BEEN CHANGED'.                   CPI00001
014100     05  ERR-MSG-13           PIC X(35)  VALUE           CPI00001
014200          'EMPLOYEE HAS BEEN ADDED'.                     CPI00001
```

```
014300        05  ERR-MSG-14             PIC X(35)        VALUE       CPI00001
014400            'EMPLOYEE NOT ON FILE'.                             CPI00001
014600*****      KEY COMPARE FIELDS                                   CPI00001
014800 01  KEY-FIELDS.                                                CPI00001
014900     05  KEY-EMPINSUM.                                          CPI00001
015000         10  KEY-EMP-JUR-ST        PIC X(2).                    CPI00001
015100         10  KEY-EMP-JUR-DIV       PIC X(3).                    CPI00001
015200         10  KEY-EMP-JUR-DEPT      PIC X(3).                    CPI00001
015300         10  KEY-EMP-NUM           PIC X(5).                    CPI00001
015400         10  KEY-EMP-NUM-R REDEFINES KEY-EMP-NUM PIC 9(5).      CPI00001
015500     05  KEY-MAINTCRD.                                          CPI00001
015600         10  KEY-MAINT-JUR-ST      PIC X(2).                    CPI00001
015700         10  KEY-MAINT-JUR-DIV     PIC X(3).                    CPI00001
015800         10  KEY-MAINT-JUR-DEPT    PIC X(3).                    CPI00001
015900         10  KEY-MAINT-EMP-NUM     PIC X(5).                    CPI00001
016100*****      LITERALS                                             CPI00001
016300 01  LIT-LITERALS.                                              CPI00001
016400     05  LIT-EMPINSUM              PIC X(32)        VALUE       CPI00001
016500            'NO OF EMPINSUM READ IS '.                          CPI00001
016600     05  LIT-EMPOUTSM              PIC X(32)        VALUE       CPI00001
016700            'NO OF EMPOUTSM WRITTEN IS '.                       CPI00001
016800     05  LIT-MAINT-ADD            PIC X(32)         VALUE       CPI00001
016900            'NO OF ADD TRANSACTIONS IS '.                       CPI00001
017000     05  LIT-MAINT-CHG            PIC X(32)         VALUE       CPI00001
017100            'NO OF CHANGE TRANSACTIONS IS '.                    CPI00001
017200     05  LIT-MAINT-DEL            PIC X(32)         VALUE       CPI00001
017300            'NO OF DELETE TRANSACTIONS IS '.                    CPI00001
017400     05  LIT-MAINT-ERR            PIC X(32)         VALUE       CPI00001
017500            'NO OF ERROR TRANSACTIONS IS '.                     CPI00001
017700*****      EMPLOYEE SUMMARY FILE                                CPI00001
017900 01  EMP-SUMMARY.                                               CPI00001
018000     05  EMP-JUR-ST               PIC X(2).                     CPI00001
018100     05  EMP-JUR-DIV              PIC X(3).                     CPI00001
018200     05  EMP-JUR-DEPT             PIC X(3).                     CPI00001
018300     05  EMP-NUM                  PIC 9(5).                     CPI00001
018400     05  EMP-NAME                 PIC X(15).                    CPI00001
018500     05  EMP-ANN-SAL              PIC S9(5)V99     COMP-3.      CPI00001
018600     05  EMP-HIRE-DATE            PIC S9(7)        COMP-3.      CPI00001
018700     05  FILLER                   PIC X(6).                     CPI00001
```

```
018900******          EMPLOYEE MAINTENANCE TRANSACTION FILE            CPI00001

019100 01  MAINT-CARD.                                                 CPI00001
019200     05  MAINT-TRANS-ID              PIC X(2).                   CPI00001
019300         88 MAINT-TRANS-ID-VALID               VALUE 'ES'.       CPI00001
019400     05  MAINT-TRANS-CODE            PIC XX.                     CPI00001
019500         88 MAINT-TRANS-DEL                    VALUE '01'.       CPI00001
019600         88 MAINT-TRANS-ADD                    VALUE '05'.       CPI00001
019700         88 MAINT-TRANS-CHG                    VALUE '09'.       CPI00001
019800     05  MAINT-JUR.                                             CPI00001
019900         10  MAINT-JUR-ST            PIC XX.                     CPI00001
020000         10  MAINT-JUR-DIV           PIC X(3).                   CPI00001
020100         10  MAINT-JUR-DEPT          PIC X(3).                   CPI00001
020200     05  MAINT-EMP-NUM               PIC X(5).                   CPI00001
020300     05  MAINT-EMP-NAME              PIC X(15).                  CPI00001
020400     05  MAINT-ANN-SAL               PIC X(7).                   CPI00001
020500     05  MAINT-ANN-SAL-R1 REDEFINES MAINT-ANN-SAL PIC 9(5)V99.  CPI00001
020600     05  MAINT-HIRE-DATE             PIC X(6).                   CPI00001
020700     05  FILLER                      PIC X(35).                  CPI00001

021000******          HEADINGS AND PRINT LINES                         CPI00001

021200 01  H1-HEADING.                                                 CPI00001
021300     05  FILLER           PIC X(5)     VALUE 'DATE'.             CPI00001
021400     05  H1-DATE          PIC X(8).                              CPI00001
021500     05  FILLER           PIC X(44)    VALUE                     CPI00001
021600                                                'EM'.            CPI00001
021700     05  FILLER     'PLOYEE SUMMARY REPORT      PIC X(44)        CPI00001
021900     05  FILLER           PIC X(24)    VALUE              '.'    CPI00001
022000     05  H1-PAGE-NO       PIC ZZ9.                               CPI00001
022100     05  FILLER           PIC X(4)     VALUE SPACES.             CPI00001

022400 01  H2-HEADING.                                                 CPI00001
022500     05  FILLER           PIC X(44)    VALUE              'F'.   CPI00001
022600     05  FILLER     'OR COMPUTER PARTNERS       PIC X(44)        CPI00001
022800     05  FILLER           PIC X(44)    VALUE              '.'    CPI00001
```

```
023200 01  PRT-LINE                      PIC X(132)          VALUE SPACES.          CPIO0001

023400 01  PR1-LINE-R1 REDEFINES PRT-LINE.                                          CPIO0001
023500     05  FILLER              PIC X(5).                                        CPIO0001
023600     05  PR1-TRANS-ID        PIC X(2).                                        CPIO0001
023700     05  FILLER              PIC X(5).                                        CPIO0001
023800     05  PR1-TRANS-CODE      PIC X(2).                                        CPIO0001
023900     05  FILLER              PIC X(5).                                        CPIO0001
024000     05  PR1-JUR-ST          PIC X(2).                                        CPIO0001
024100     05  FILLER              PIC X(3).                                        CPIO0001
024200     05  PR1-JUR-DIV         PIC X.                                           CPIO0001
024300     05  FILLER              PIC X(3).                                        CPIO0001
024400     05  PR1-JUR-DEPT        PIC X(5).                                        CPIO0001
024500     05  FILLER              PIC X(5).                                        CPIO0001
024600     05  PR1-EMP-NUM         PIC X(5).                                        CPIO0001
024700     05  FILLER              PIC X(15).                                       CPIO0001
024800     05  PR1-EMP-NAME        PIC X(5).                                        CPIO0001
024900     05  FILLER              PIC X(7).                                        CPIO0001
025000     05  PR1-ANN-SAL         PIC X(5).                                        CPIO0001
025100     05  FILLER              PIC X(6).                                        CPIO0001
025200     05  PR1-HIRE-DATE       PIC X(5).                                        CPIO0001
025300     05  FILLER              PIC X(5).                                        CPIO0001
025400     05  PR1-ERR-MSG         PIC X(5).                                        CPIO0001

025600******   SWITCHES                                                            CPIO0001

025800 01  SW-SWITCHES.                                                             CPIO0001
025900     05  SW-EDIT-TRANS       PIC X           VALUE '1'.                       CPIO0001
026000         88 SW-EDIT-TRANS-VALID              VALUE '0'.                       CPIO0001
026100         88 SW-EDIT-TRANS-INVALID            VALUE '1'.                       CPIO0001
```

```
026300 PROCEDURE DIVISION.                                                       CPI00001

026500 0000-DRIVER.                                                              CPI00001

026700*****       INITIALIZATION LOGIC                                           CPI00001

026900        OPEN INPUT EMPINSUM-FILE                                           CPI00001
027000                   MAINTCRD-FILE                                           CPI00001
027100             OUTPUT EMPOUTSM-FILE                                          CPI00001
027200                    REPTEMPS-FILE.                                         CPI00001
027300        PERFORM 3000-READ-EMPINSUM THRU 3099-EXIT.                         CPI00001
027400        PERFORM 3400-READ-MAINTCRD THRU 3499-EXIT.                         CPI00001
027500        PERFORM 4000-EDIT-MAINTCRD THRU 4099-EXIT                          CPI00001
027600            UNTIL SW-EDIT-TRANS-VALID.                                     CPI00001
027700        MOVE CURRENT-DATE TO HI-DATE.                                      CPI00001

027900*****       DRIVER CONTROLS PROCESSING OF INPUT                            CPI00001
028000*****       UNTIL END OF FILE IS REACHED ON BOTH FILES                     CPI00001

028200        PERFORM 1000-PROCESS-INPUT THRU 1099-EXIT                          CPI00001
028300            UNTIL KEY-EMPINSUM EQUAL TO HIGH-VALUES AND                     CPI00001
028400                  KEY-MAINTCRD EQUAL TO HIGH-VALUES.                       CPI00001

028600*****       END OF JOB LOGIC                                               CPI00001

028800        DISPLAY LIT-EMPINSUM  CNT-EMPINSUM.                                CPI00001
028900        DISPLAY LIT-EMPOUTSM  CNT-EMPOUTSM.                                CPI00001
029000        DISPLAY LIT-MAINT-ADD CNT-MAINT-ADD.                               CPI00001
029100        DISPLAY LIT-MAINT-CHG CNT-MAINT-CHG.                               CPI00001
029200        DISPLAY LIT-MAINT-DEL CNT-MAINT-DEL.                               CPI00001
029300        DISPLAY LIT-MAINT-ERR CNT-MAINT-ERR.                               CPI00001
029400        CLOSE EMPINSUM-FILE                                                CPI00001
029500              EMPOUTSM-FILE                                                CPI00001
029600              MAINTCRD-FILE                                                CPI00001
029700              REPTEMPS-FILE.                                               CPI00001
029800        GOBACK.
```

78

```
030000******    MAIN PROCESSING LOGIC - PERFORMS FILE MATCH        CPI00001

030200 1000-PROCESS-INPUT.                                         CPI00001

030400     IF KEY-MAINTCRD GREATER THAN KEY-EMPINSUM              CPI00001
030500        PERFORM 3100-WRITE-EMPOUTSM THRU 3199-EXIT          CPI00001
030600        PERFORM 3000-READ-EMPINSUM  THRU 3099-EXIT          CPI00001
030700        GO TO 1099-EXIT.                                    CPI00001

030900******    IF INPUT TRANSACTION MATCHES EMPLOYEE ON FILE,     CPI00001
031000******    PROCESS CHANGE OR DELETE (ADD IS ERROR).          CPI00001

031200     IF KEY-MAINTCRD EQUAL TO KEY-EMPINSUM                  CPI00001
031300        IF MAINT-TRANS-CHG                                  CPI00001
031400        ELSE PERFORM 2000-UPDATE-EMPLOYEE THRU 2099-EXIT    CPI00001
031500        ELSE                                                CPI00001
031600           IF MAINT-TRANS-DEL                               CPI00001
031700              PERFORM 2100-DELETE-EMPLOYEE THRU 2199-EXIT   CPI00001
031800           ELSE                                             CPI00001
031900              MOVE ERR-MSG-01 TO PR1-ERR-MSG.               CPI00001

032100     IF KEY-MAINTCRD LESS THAN KEY-EMPINSUM                 CPI00001
032200        IF MAINT-TRANS-ADD                                  CPI00001
032300        ELSE PERFORM 2300-ADD-EMPLOYEE THRU 2399-EXIT       CPI00001
032400        ELSE                                                CPI00001
032500           MOVE ERR-MSG-14 TO PR1-ERR-MSG.                  CPI00001

032700******    WRITE-REPORT LINE AND                             CPI00001
032800******    READ AND EDIT NEXT INPUT TRANSACTION              CPI00001

033000     PERFORM 3200-WRITE-A-LINE THRU 3299-EXIT.              CPI00001
033100     PERFORM 3400-READ-MAINTCRD THRU 3499-EXIT.             CPI00001
033200     PERFORM 4000-EDIT-MAINTCRD THRU 4099-EXIT              CPI00001
033300        UNTIL SW-EDIT-TRANS-VALID.                          CPI00001

033500 1099-EXIT.                                                 CPI00001
033600     EXIT.                                                  CPI00001
```

79

```
033800******        UPDATE THE EMPLOYEE RECORD                    CPI00001
033900******        FROM THE MAINTENANCE TRANSACTION              CPI00001

034100 2000-UPDATE-EMPLOYEE.                                      CPI00001

034300     IF MAINT-EMP-NAME NOT EQUAL SPACE                      CPI00001
034400        MOVE MAINT-EMP-NAME TO EMP-NAME.                    CPI00001
034500     IF MAINT-ANN-SAL NOT EQUAL SPACE                       CPI00001
034600        MOVE MAINT-ANN-SAL-R1 TO EMP-ANN-SAL.               CPI00001
034700     IF MAINT-HIRE-DATE NOT EQUAL SPACE                     CPI00001
034800        MOVE MAINT-HIRE-DATE TO EMP-HIRE-DATE.              CPI00001
034900     PERFORM 3100-WRITE-EMPOUTSM THRU 3199-EXIT.            CPI00001
035000     ADD +1 TO CNT-MAINT-CHG.                               CPI00001
035100     PERFORM 3000-READ-EMPINSUM THRU 3099-EXIT.             CPI00001
035200     MOVE ERR-MSG-12 TO PRI-ERR-MSG.                        CPI00001

035400 2099-EXIT.                                                 CPI00001
035500     EXIT.                                                  CPI00001


035700******        DELETE EMPLOYEE FROM SUMMARY FILE             CPI00001

035900 2100-DELETE-EMPLOYEE.                                      CPI00001

036100     PERFORM 3000-READ-EMPINSUM THRU 3099-EXIT.            CPI00001
036200     ADD +1 TO CNT-MAINT-DEL.                               CPI00001
036300     MOVE ERR-MSG-11 TO PRI-ERR-MSG.                        CPI00001

036500 2199-EXIT.                                                 CPI00001
036600     EXIT.                                                  CPI00001
```

```
036800*****      ADD A NEW EMPLOYEE TO THE SUMMARY FILE        CPIO0001

037000 2300-ADD-EMPLOYEE.                                       CPIO0001

037200     MOVE MAINT-JUR-ST TO EMP-JUR-ST.                     CPIO0001
037300     MOVE MAINT-JUR-DIV TO EMP-JUR-DIV.                   CPIO0001
037400     MOVE MAINT-JUR-DEPT TO EMP-JUR-DEPT.                 CPIO0001
037500     MOVE MAINT-EMP-NUM TO EMP-NUM.                       CPIO0001
037600     MOVE MAINT-EMP-NAME TO EMP-NAME.                     CPIO0001
037700     MOVE MAINT-ANN-SAL-RI TO EMP-ANN-SAL.                CPIO0001
037800     MOVE MAINT-HIRE-DATE TO EMP-HIRE-DATE.               CPIO0001
037900     PERFORM 3100-WRITE-EMPOUTSM THRU 3199-EXIT.          CPIO0001
038000     ADD +1 TO CNT-MAINT-ADD.                             CPIO0001
038100     MOVE ERR-MSG-13 TO PR1-ERR-MSG.                      CPIO0001

038300 2399-EXIT.                                               CPIO0001
038400     EXIT.                                                CPIO0001
```

81

```
038600******    READ THE NEXT INPUT EMPLOYEE SUMMARY RECORD       CPI00001

038800 3000-READ-EMPINSUM.                                        CPI00001

039000     READ EMPINSUM-FILE INTO EMP-SUMMARY                    CPI00001
039100         AT END                                             CPI00001
039200             MOVE HIGH-VALUES TO KEY-EMPINSUM               CPI00001
039300             GO TO 3099-EXIT.                               CPI00001
039400     ADD +1 TO CNT-EMPINSUM.                                CPI00001
039500     MOVE EMP-JUR-ST TO KEY-EMP-JUR-ST.                     CPI00001
039600     MOVE EMP-JUR-DIV TO KEY-EMP-JUR-DIV.                   CPI00001
039700     MOVE EMP-JUR-DEPT TO KEY-EMP-JUR-DEPT.                 CPI00001
039800     MOVE EMP-NUM TO KEY-EMP-NUM-R.                         CPI00001

040000 3099-EXIT.                                                 CPI00001
040100     EXIT.                                                  CPI00001


040300******    WRITE AN EMPLOYEE SUMMARY RECORD                  CPI00001

040500 3100-WRITE-EMPOUTSM.                                       CPI00001

040700     WRITE EMPOUTSM-REC FROM EMP-SUMMARY.                   CPI00001
040800     ADD +1 TO CNT-EMPOUTSM.                                CPI00001

041000 3199-EXIT.                                                 CPI00001
041100     EXIT.                                                  CPI00001
```

```
041300******        PRINT HEADINGS AND REPORT LINES          CPI00001

041500 3200-WRITE-A-LINE.                                     CPI00001

041700        MOVE '1' TO SW-EDIT-TRANS.                      CPI00001
041800        IF CNT-LINES LESS THAN CNT-LINE-LIMIT           CPI00001
041900            GO TO 3250-DETAIL.                          CPI00001
042000        ADD +1 TO CNT-PAGES.                            CPI00001
042100        MOVE CNT-PAGES TO H1-PAGE-NO.                   CPI00001
042200        MOVE H1-HEADING TO REPT-PRT-LINE.               CPI00001
042300        MOVE '1' TO REPT-CTL-CHAR.                      CPI00001
042400        PERFORM 3300-WRITE-REPTEMPS THRU 3399-EXIT.     CPI00001
042500        MOVE H2-HEADING TO REPT-PRT-LINE.               CPI00001
042600        MOVE '0' TO REPT-CTL-CHAR.                      CPI00001
042700        PERFORM 3300-WRITE-REPTEMPS THRU 3399-EXIT.     CPI00001
042800        MOVE '0' TO REPT-CTL-CHAR.                      CPI00001

043000 3250-DETAIL.                                           CPI00001

043200        MOVE PRT-LINE TO REPT-PRT-LINE.                 CPI00001
043300        PERFORM 3300-WRITE-REPTEMPS THRU 3399-EXIT.     CPI00001
043400        MOVE SPACES TO PRT-LINE.                        CPI00001
043500        MOVE SPACE TO REPT-CTL-CHAR.                    CPI00001

043700 3299-EXIT.                                             CPI00001
043800        EXIT.                                           CPI00001

044000******        WRITE A LINE ON REPTEMPS-FILE             CPI00001

044200 3300-WRITE-REPTEMPS.                                   CPI00001

044400        WRITE REPTEMPS-REC AFTER POSITIONING REPT-CTL-CHAR.  CPI00001
044500        IF REPT-CTL-CHAR EQUAL ' '                      CPI00001
044600            ADD +1 TO CNT-LINES                         CPI00001
044700            GO TO 3399-EXIT.                            CPI00001
044800        IF REPT-CTL-CHAR EQUAL '0'                      CPI00001
044900            ADD +2 TO CNT-LINES                         CPI00001
045000            GO TO 3399-EXIT.                            CPI00001
045100        IF REPT-CTL-CHAR EQUAL '-'                      CPI00001
045200            ADD +3 TO CNT-LINES                         CPI00001
045300            GO TO 3399-EXIT.                            CPI00001
045400        MOVE +1 TO CNT-LINES.                           CPI00001

045600 3399-EXIT.                                             CPI00001
045700        EXIT.                                           CPI00001
```

```
045900******      READ THE NEXT INPUT MAINTENANCE TRANSACTION      CPI00001

046100 3400-READ-MAINTCRD.                                         CPI00001

046300     READ MAINTCRD-FILE INTO MAINT-CARD                      CPI00001
046400         AT END                                              CPI00001
046500             MOVE HIGH-VALUES  TO KEY-MAINTCRD               CPI00001
046600             GO TO 3499-EXIT.                                CPI00001
046700     ADD +1 TO CNT-MAINT-CRD.                                CPI00001
046800     MOVE MAINT-JUR-ST     TO  KEY-MAINT-JUR-ST.             CPI00001
046900     MOVE MAINT-JUR-DIV    TO  KEY-MAINT-JUR-DIV.            CPI00001
047000     MOVE MAINT-JUR-DEPT   TO  KEY-MAINT-JUR-DEPT.           CPI00001
047100     MOVE MAINT-EMP-NUM    TO  KEY-MAINT-EMP-NUM.            CPI00001
047200     MOVE MAINT-JUR-ST     TO  PRI-JUR-ST                    CPI00001
047300     MOVE MAINT-TRANS-ID   TO  PRI-TRANS-ID.                 CPI00001
047400     MOVE MAINT-TRANS-CODE TO  PRI-TRANS-CODE.               CPI00001
047500     MOVE MAINT-JUR-DIV    TO  PRI-JUR-DIV.                  CPI00001
047600     MOVE MAINT-JUR-DEPT   TO  PRI-JUR-DEPT.                 CPI00001
047700     MOVE MAINT-EMP-NUM    TO  PRI-EMP-NUM.                  CPI00001
047800     MOVE MAINT-EMP-NAME   TO  PRI-EMP-NAME.                 CPI00001
047900     MOVE MAINT-ANN-SAL    TO  PRI-ANN-SAL.                  CPI00001
048000     MOVE MAINT-HIRE-DATE  TO  PRI-HIRE-DATE.                CPI00001

048200 3499-EXIT.                                                  CPI00001
048300     EXIT.                                                   CPI00001
```

```
048500******           EDIT THE INPUT MAINTENANCE TRANSACTION                CPI00001
048600******           LIST ALL ERRORS                                       CPI00001
                                                                             CPI00001
048800 4000-EDIT-MAINTCRD.                                                   CPI00001
049000     MOVE '0' TO SW-EDIT-TRANS.                                        CPI00001
049100     IF NOT MAINT-TRANS-ID-VALID                                       CPI00001
049200         MOVE ERR-MSG-02 TO PR1-ERR-MSG                                CPI00001
049300         PERFORM 3200-WRITE-A-LINE THRU 3299-EXIT.                     CPI00001
049400     IF NOT MAINT-TRANS-ADD                                           CPI00001
049500         AND NOT MAINT-TRANS-DEL                                       CPI00001
049600         AND NOT MAINT-TRANS-CHG                                       CPI00001
049700         MOVE ERR-MSG-03 TO PR1-ERR-MSG                                CPI00001
049800         PERFORM 3200-WRITE-A-LINE THRU 3299-EXIT.                     CPI00001
049900     IF MAINT-JUR-ST NOT NUMERIC                                       CPI00001
050000         MOVE ERR-MSG-04 TO PR1-ERR-MSG                                CPI00001
050100         PERFORM 3200-WRITE-A-LINE THRU 3299-EXIT.                     CPI00001
050200     IF MAINT-JUR-DIV NOT NUMERIC                                      CPI00001
050300         MOVE ERR-MSG-05 TO PR1-ERR-MSG                                CPI00001
050400         PERFORM 3200-WRITE-A-LINE THRU 3299-EXIT.                     CPI00001
050500     IF MAINT-JUR-DEPT NOT NUMERIC                                     CPI00001
050600         MOVE ERR-MSG-06 TO PR1-ERR-MSG                                CPI00001
050700         PERFORM 3200-WRITE-A-LINE THRU 3299-EXIT.                     CPI00001
050800     IF MAINT-EMP-NUM NOT NUMERIC                                      CPI00001
050900         MOVE ERR-MSG-07 TO PR1-ERR-MSG                                CPI00001
051000         PERFORM 3200-WRITE-A-LINE THRU 3299-EXIT.                     CPI00001
051100     IF MAINT-TRANS-ADD AND MAINT-EMP-NAME EQUAL SPACE                 CPI00001
051200         MOVE ERR-MSG-08 TO PR1-ERR-MSG                                CPI00001
051300         PERFORM 3200-WRITE-A-LINE THRU 3299-EXIT.                     CPI00001
051400     IF MAINT-TRANS-ADD AND MAINT-ANN-SAL-R1 NOT NUMERIC              CPI00001
051500         MOVE ERR-MSG-09 TO PR1-ERR-MSG                                CPI00001
051600         PERFORM 3200-WRITE-A-LINE THRU 3299-EXIT.                     CPI00001
051700     IF MAINT-TRANS-CHG                                               CPI00001
051800         AND MAINT-ANN-SAL NOT EQUAL SPACE                            CPI00001
051900         AND MAINT-ANN-SAL-R1 NOT NUMERIC                             CPI00001
052000         MOVE ERR-MSG-09 TO PR1-ERR-MSG                                CPI00001
052100         PERFORM 3200-WRITE-A-LINE THRU 3299-EXIT.                     CPI00001
052200     IF MAINT-TRANS-ADD                                               CPI00001
052300         AND MAINT-HIRE-DATE NOT NUMERIC                              CPI00001
052400         MOVE ERR-MSG-10 TO PR1-ERR-MSG                                CPI00001
052500         PERFORM 3200-WRITE-A-LINE THRU 3299-EXIT.                     CPI00001
052600     IF MAINT-TRANS-CHG                                               CPI00001
052700         AND MAINT-HIRE-DATE NOT EQUAL TO SPACE                       CPI00001
052800         AND MAINT-HIRE-DATE NOT NUMERIC                              CPI00001
052900         MOVE ERR-MSG-10 TO PR1-ERR-MSG                                CPI00001
053000         PERFORM 3200-WRITE-A-LINE THRU 3299-EXIT.                     CPI00001
```

```
053100     IF SW-EDIT-TRANS-INVALID                              CPI00001
053200         PERFORM 3400-READ-MAINTCRD THRU 3499-EXIT.        CPI00001
053400 4099-EXIT.                                                CPI00001
053500     EXIT.                                                 CPI00001
```

IX.
DATA
DIVISION
— IMS

Many of the standards recommended for the data division of non-IMS programs also apply to IMS programs. All data elements which are not directly related to IMS processing (e.g., switches, accumulators) will conform to standards discussed in that section. IMS (DB and/or DC) programming utilizes several special purpose areas in both the working storage and linkage sections and consideration must be given to unique naming conventions, formatting conventions, and organization of these areas.

Since data sharing is inherent to the IMS data base concept, consistent description of shared data among using programs is of utmost importance. The use of common source or copy library members for segments, messages, search arguments, program control block masks, and other IMS-related data is strongly recommended. Under no circumstances should an application program use self-defined segment or message field descriptions. By also providing common source code for search arguments, PCBs, function codes, command codes, and status codes, a great deal of redundant coding can be eliminated. This not only standardizes the coding, but also reduces the likelihood of error.

A.   WORKING STORAGE SECTION

The consistent organization and naming of data areas for IMS-related fields in the working storage section is critical to the coding of an understandable and readable program. A program which is both readable and understandable will also be more reliable, since, as complexity increases, errors tend to increase. In a data base environment, either batch or on-line, program errors have more impact since they may affect the integrity of the shared data base. Therefore, any measures which can be taken to decrease complexity and increase reliability should be taken. One of those measures, again, is the use of common source or copy library members for data areas in working storage.

1. SEGMENT AREAS

If one of the data dictionary software packages is being used, segment descriptions will be generated by the data dictionary and will be placed, usually, in a COBOL copy library. If there is no data dictionary, then each segment description should be placed on a source or copy library for use by all programs.

Each source or copy member describing a data base segment should also include comments documenting the format and specifying the data base name, the segment name from the data base definition, the actual length in bytes of the segment, a date or version stamp, and a brief description of the segment.

```
*******************************************
*      DBDNAME = EMPPAYDB                  *
*      SEGNAME = EMPLOYEE                   *
*      LENGTH  = 108                        *
*      DATE    = 09/16/80                   *
*      DESC:   EMPLOYEE ID FOR PAYROLL      *
*******************************************
```

Segments and the fields within them should be assigned
names which are descriptive and reasonably brief.
Names should conform to the following conventions:

a. The 01-level segment name should begin with a
    meaningful prefix taken from the segment name in
    the data base definition (e.g., EMP for the
    EMPLOYEE segment).

b. The prefix should be followed with a data base
    identifier (e.g., EMP-PAYROLL).

c. The 01-level should be suffixed with 'SEG' to
    identify it as a segment (e.g., 01 EMP-PAYROLL-SEG).

d. All data names within the segment should consist
    of the segment name prefix plus a meaningful name
    and an optional suffix to indicate a special
    function (e.g., 05 EMP-K-SOCSEC).

Segment descriptions coded for a source or copy
library should always match the segment as it physically exists on the data base. In other words, do not
allow filler at the end of a source description which
is not physically present in the segment. Doing so
could result in alignment problems when using path
calls.

2. MESSAGE AREAS

    Transaction input and output areas in message process-
    ing programs should be named so that their function
    and related transaction code(s) are apparent.

    a. There should always be one input area and one out-
        put area named MSG-IN-AREA and MSG-OUT-AREA,
        respectively.

    b. The input and output areas should each be rede-
        fined with message formats for transactions
        received or sent by the program.

    c. Each message description should include in the
        01-level name the actual transaction code, the
        literal 'MSG', an optional literal 'SEGM' for seg-
        mented messages, and a suffix of 'IN' or 'OUT'.

```
01   MSG-IN-AREA                      PIC X(400).
01   TRANCD01-MSG-IN    REDEFINES MSG-IN-AREA.
```

NOTE: If the above naming conventions are
        followed, source or copy library entries may
        continue to be used for message descrip-
        tions, even though they use the REDEFINES
        clause, since the input and output area
        names are standard.

d. All fields within the message should be named with
    the transaction code, the literal 'IN' or 'OUT',
    and a descriptive name (e.g., TRANCD01-IN-EMPNO).

e. All attribute byte fields in output messages
    should be the field name suffixed with 'ATTR'.

f. All fields in input messages which can be entered
    by the terminal operator should be defined as
    alphanumeric (PIC X instead of PIC 9).

3. SEGMENT SEARCH ARGUMENTS

    Two segment search argument masks should be maintained
    on a copy or source library for each data base
    segment. There will be one qualified search argument
    (assuming the segment is keyed) and one unqualified.

    a. Arguments should be given the same name as the
        segment description, and suffixed with 'USSA' or
        'QSSA' instead of 'SEG'   (e.g., 01 EMP-PAY-
        ROLL-USSA).

    b. Individual fields within the argument should be
        named only if they will be referenced by the
        program; otherwise they should be designated as
        FILLER. Command code fields should be suffixed
        with 'Ccn'. The relational operator should be
        suffixed with 'OPER'. The key field should be
        suffixed with 'KEY-VAL'.

```
01  EMP-PAYROLL-USSA.
    05  FILLER              PIC X(9) VALUE 'EMPLOYEE*'.
    05  EMP-U-CC1           PIC X    VALUE '-'.
    05  EMP-U-CC2           PIC X    VALUE '-'.
    05  FILLER              PIC X    VALUE SPACE.
01  EMP-PAYROLL-QSSA.
    05  FILLER              PIC X(9) VALUE 'EMPLOYEE*'.
    05  EMP-Q-CC1           PIC X    VALUE '-'.
    05  EMP-Q-CC2           PIC X    VALUE '-'.
    05  FILLER              PIC X(9) VALUE '(EMPNUMBR'.
    05  EMP-Q-OPER          PIC X    VALUE '='.
    05  EMP-Q-KEY-VAL       PIC X(9).
    05  FILLER              PIC X    VALUE ')'.
```

c. Two command codes should be defined in each search argument. They should be initialized to the null ('-') command code value.

If specialized search arguments are needed, for Boolean operations or requests on search instead of key fields, the using program should set up a unique search argument. In the case of a Boolean search which combines key and search fields, key fields should precede search fields in the argument.

4. FUNCTION CODES

A common source member should be set up to define all IMS function codes as variables. Each variable should be named descriptively and prefixed with 'FUNC'.

```
01  IMS FUNCTION-CODES.
    05  FUNC-GET-UNIQUE                 PIC X(4) VALUE 'GU  '.
    05  FUNC-GET-NEXT                   PIC X(4) VALUE 'GN  '.
    05  FUNC-GET-HOLD-UNIQUE            PIC X(4) VALUE 'GHU '.
    05  FUNC-GET-HOLD-NEXT              PIC X(4) VALUE 'GHN '.
    05  FUNC-GET-NEXT-WITHIN-PARENT     PIC X(4) VALUE 'GHP '.
    05  FUNC-GET-HOLD-NEXT-PARENT       PIC X(4) VALUE 'GHNP'.
    05  FUNC-INSERT                     PIC X(4) VALUE 'ISRT'.
    05  FUNC-REPLACE                    PIC X(4) VALUE 'REPL'.
    05  FUNC-DELETE                     PIC X(4) VALUE 'DLET'.
    05  FUNC-CHECKPOINT                 PIC X(4) VALUE 'CHKP'.
    05  FUNC-PURGE                      PIC X(4) VALUE 'PURG'.
    05  FUNC-CHANGE                     PIC X(4) VALUE 'CHNG'.
    05  FUNC-RESTART                    PIC X(4) VALUE 'XRST'.
    05  FUNC-STAT                       PIC X(4) VALUE 'STAT'.
    05  FUNC-SNAP                       PIC X(4) VALUE 'SNAP'.
    05  FUNC-LOG                        PIC X(4) VALUE 'LOG '.
```

5. COMMAND CODES

A common copy or source library member should define IMS command codes. Names should be descriptive and end in the word 'COMMAND'.

```
01  IMS-COMMAND-CODES.
    05  CMND-PATH                PIC X    VALUE 'D'.
    05  CMND-PARENT              PIC X    VALUE 'P'.
    05  CMND-FIRST               PIC X    VALUE 'F'.
    05  CMND-LAST                PIC X    VALUE 'L'.
    05  CMND-NOREPLACE           PIC X    VALUE 'N'.
    05  CMND-POSITION            PIC X    VALUE 'U'.
    05  CMND-PATH-POSITION       PIC X    VALUE 'V'.
    05  CMND-NULL                PIC X    VALUE '-'.
    05  CMND-CONCAT-KEY          PIC X    VALUE 'C'.
```

6. Data names with values should be defined for all
common attribute byte combinations. The attribute
definitions should be available as a source or copy
library member. All attribute field names should be
suffixed with 'ATTR'.

```
01  ATTRIBUTE-BYTE-DATA    COMP.
    05  VALUE1                      PIC S9(8) VALUE +128.
    05  FILLER       REDEFINES VALUE1.
        10  FILLER                  PIC XX.
        10  ATTR-NUM-PROT-H1-MOD   PIC XX.
    05  VALUE2                      PIC S9(8) VALUE +136.
    05  FILLER       REDEFINES VALUE2.
        10  FILLER                  PIC XX.
        10  ATTR-ALPHA-PROT-NORM-MOD PIC XX.
```

B.   <u>LINKAGE SECTION</u>

The linkage section of an IMS program must conform to
specific conventions. The order of program control block
masks is determined outside of the application program,
but PCB's in the linkage section should be in the same
order as they appear on the ENTRY statement. Names of the
data areas are assigned by the application program and
should be chosen in a consistent manner.

Program control block masks should be named as follows:

a. Data base PCB names should be defined with a generic
prefix which is recognizable as defining the data base
in question, for example EMP-PAY-PCB.

b. All fields within the PCB should be prefixed with a
generic prefix that is a descriptive indication of the
data base, and be suffixed with the standard field
names used in the following example:

```
01  EMP-PAY-PCB
    05  EMP-PAY-DBDNAME          PIC X(8).
    05  EMP-PAY-LEVEL            PIC XX.
    05  EMP-PAY-STATUS-CODE      PIC XX.
        88  EMP-SUCCESSFUL-CALL  VALUE SPACES.
        88  EMP-SEG-NOT-FOUND    VALUE 'GE'.
        88  EMP-END-OF-DB        VALUE 'GB'.
        88  EMP-LEVEL-CHANGE     VALUE 'GA'.
        88  EMP-SEG-CHANGE       VALUE 'GK'.
        88  EMP-DUPLICATE-KEY    VALUE 'II'.
    05  EMP-PAY-PROCOPT          PIC X(4).
    05  EMP-PAY-RESV             PIC S9(5) COMP.
    05  EMP-PAY-SEGNAME          PIC X(8).
    05  EMP-PAY-KEYLEN           PIC S9(5) COMP.
    05  EMP-PAY-SENSEG           PIC S9(5) COMP.
    05  EMP-PAY-KEYFB            PIC X(N).
```

All "normal" status codes should be descriptively
defined as 88 level values in the PCB definition, in
order to avoid checking literal values in the procedure division. "Normal" status codes are those which
may be logically processed by the program. "Abnormal"
status codes are those for which corrective action is
beyond control of the program and for which abnormal
termination should be forced.

The key feedback area should be redefined by the program
as many times as necessary to describe each hierarchical
path in the logical view.

c. The input/output control block for message processing
   programs should always be named 'IO-PCB'. Fields
   within this PCB should have the following names:

```
01  IO-PCB.
    05  IO-LTERM               PIC X(8).
    05  IO-RESV                PIC XX.
    05  IO-STATUS-CODE         PIC XX.
        88  IO-SUCCESSFUL-CALL VALUE SPACES.
        88  IO-NO-MESSAGES     VALUE 'QC'.
        88  IO-NO-MSG-SEGMENTS VALUE 'QD'.
    05  IO-JULDATE             PIC S9(7) COMP-3.
    05  IO-TIME                PIC S9(7) COMP-3.
    05  IO-MSG-SEQ             PIC S9(7) COMP.
    05  IO-MODNAME             PIC X(8).
    05  IO-OPER-ID             PIC X(8).
```

d. Alternate terminal PCBs should have an 01-level name
   of 'ALTn-PCB', where 'n' is a unique numeric identifier. Field names within the PCB should also begin
   with 'ALTn' and they should have the same descriptive
   names as the IO-PCB fields.

e. Alternate modifiable PCBs should be named 'ALTMn-PCB',
   where 'n' is again a unique numeric identifier. Field
   names should be prefixed with 'ALTMn'.

X.
PROCEDURE
DIVISION — IMS

A.   LOGICAL ORGANIZATION

1. PROGRAM STRUCTURE

Many programs which process IMS data bases or transactions have similar requirements and, consequently,
should have a similar organization. Recognizing these
similarities and translating them into generalized
program structures for the "driver" or "mainline" will
aid in generating more consistent, understandable, and
reliable code.

Any program, IMS or not, should have a chart or
diagram, indicating either flow or structure or both,
completed prior to the start of any coding. This
chart or diagram may then serve as a "model" of the
solution to the programming problem. It will also
function as a communications tool for the analyst and
programmer since a picture often is "worth a thousand
words." Many potential questions and misunderstand-
ings can be avoided by a careful review of the program's planned structure.

An IMS batch program will frequently resemble a
non-IMS batch program if the data base(s) involved are
simply viewed as "files" (albeit a special type of
file). Standard two-file update logic (see Subroutine
Logic - Sequential File Maintenance) or report-writing
logic may be used in those applications which are data
base driven (e.g., their processing is controlled by
the sequential access of data base root segments).

An IMS batch program which is transaction-driven,
(i.e., accesses the data base in a "get-unique" or
"look-up" mode) - should be organized in such a way
that the main processing logic is executed once per
transaction. The following sample illustrates the
skeleton code for a transaction driven program.

```
0000-DRIVER.

*****      INITIALIZATION

        OPEN INPUT   TRAN-FILE
             OUTPUT REPORT-FILE.
        MOVE CURRENT-DATE TO HDG1-DATE.
        PERFORM 4000-READ-TRANSACTION THRU 4099-EXIT.
```

```
*****       DRIVER CONTROLS PROCESSING OF
*****       TRANSACTIONS UNTIL END-OF-FILE

        PERFORM 1000-PROCESS-TRANSACTION THRU 1099-EXIT
            UNTIL NO-MORE-TRANSACTIONS
            OR IMS-ERROR-OCCURRED.

*****       END OF JOB
        PERFORM 9600-DISPLAY-TOTALS THRU 9699-EXIT.
        GOBACK.

*****       MAIN PROCESSING LOGIC

1000-PROCESS-TRANSACTION.

        MOVE TRAN-REC-KEY TO ROOT-Q-KEY-VAL.
        PERFORM 5000-GET-UNIQUE-ROOT THRU 5099-EXIT.
        IF SW-ROOT-FOUND
            PERFORM 4500-UPDATE THRU 4599-EXIT.
        ELSE
            PERFORM 4600-ADD-SEG THRU 4699-EXIT.
        PERFORM 4000-READ-TRANSACTION THRU 4099-EXIT.

1099-EXIT.
        EXIT.
```

An IMS message processing program will usually be
similar in structure to the batch transaction-driven
program. However, the source of the input is an IMS
message queue instead of an OS file, and the program
must be constructed so that it is serially reusable.
A serially reusable module is one which can be
executed a number of times in succession without
returning control to the program or operating system
which called it. For a COBOL program, this implies
that working storage areas such as switches and accumulators must be initialized prior to each loop through
the main processing logic. A message processing
program, then, should not use the VALUE clause to
provide a default value (unless that value may not be
modified), but should use the MOVE statement to assign
initial values.

An example of the driver and main processing logic for
a message processing program is shown below.

```
0000-DRIVER.
        PERFORM 1000-PROCESS-REQUEST THRU 1099-EXIT
            UNTIL NO-MORE-MESSAGES.
        GOBACK.

1000-PROCESS-REQUEST.
```

```
*****     THE MAIN PROCESSING LOGIC IS
*****     EXECUTED ONCE PER MESSAGE

     PERFORM 9000-INITIALIZATION THRU 9099-EXIT.
     PERFORM 4000-GET-MESSAGE THRU 4099-EXIT.
     IF MESSAGE-RECEIVED
         PERFORM 5000-PROCESS-MESSAGE THRU 5099-EXIT.
         PERFORM 6000-SEND-RESPONSE THRU 6099-EXIT.
 1099-EXIT.
     EXIT.
```

A batch message processing (BMP) program may usually
be classified by its primary processing objective,
either (1) to process messages which have accumulated
on the queue, (2) to place messages on the message
queue, or (3) to process against a data base which is
allocated to the IMS control region. Therefore, one
of the logic skeletons outlined above will usually
serve the purpose of a BMP.

2. ISOLATION OF FUNCTION

The phrase "isolation of function" really has two
meanings. First, it indicates a separation of
function, or, in other words, the concept of one
function per routine. A program should be organized
such that the purpose of each routine within it can be
stated in a single, simple sentence. (Ideally, that
sentence will be included as a comment preceding the
routine!) For example, each program which accesses a
data base should include one separate routine for each
type of call against each type of segment.

```
*****     THIS ROUTINE READS THE NEXT SEQUENTIAL ROOT
*****     ON THE DATA BASE FOR UPDATE

 6000-GET-NEXT-ROOT.
     CALL 'CBLTDLI' USING FUNC-GET-NEXT
                          PCB1-EMPPAYDB
                          EMP-PAYROLL-SEG
                          EMP-PAYROLL-USSA.
     IF EMP-PAY-SUCCESSFUL-CALL
         GO TO 6099-EXIT
     ELSE
         IF EMP-PAY-END-OF-DB
             MOVE LIT-END-DB TO SW-END-DATA-BASE
         ELSE
             PERFORM 8000-IMS-DB-ERROR THRU 8099-EXIT.
 6099-EXIT.
     EXIT.
```

```
*****     THIS ROUTINE READS THE NEXT SEQUENTIAL ROOT
*****     ON THE DATA BASE FOR UPDATE

   6100-GET-HOLD-ROOT.
       CALL 'CBLTDLI' USING FUNC-GET-HOLD-NEXT
                            PCB1-EMPPAYDB
                            EMP-PAYROLL-SEG
                            EMP-PAYROLL-USSA.
       IF EMP-PAY-SUCCESSFUL-CALL
           GO TO 6099-EXIT
       ELSE
           IF EMP-PAY-END-OF-DB
               MOVE LIT-END-DB TO SW-END-DATA-BASE
           ELSE
               PERFORM 8000-IMS-DB-ERROR THRU 8099-EXIT.
   6199-EXIT.
       EXIT.
```

Routines which are logically related (such as the call
routines above) by similarity of function may be
physically related by the paragraph numbering conventions and contiguous placement.

Other functions which can and should be isolated
include standard error processing, checkpoint/reposi-
tion, and handling of multi-segment messages.

The second meaning of "isolation of function" implies
defensive programming. Any common data areas or
function codes (e.g., switches, command codes) should
be set to the desired value and reset to the default
value by the using routine. For example, command
codes would be explicitly set by a routine doing a
path call and would be reset to the null value after
executing the call.

```
   6000-GET-PATH.
       MOVE CMND-PATH TO EMP-U-CC1
                         PROJ-U-CC1.
       MOVE CMND-LAST TO BILL-U-CC1.
       CALL 'CBLTDLI' USING FUNC-GET-NEXT
                            PCB1-EMPPAYDB
                            PATH-IO AREA
                            EMP-PAYROLL-USSA
                            PROJ-PAYROLL-USSA
                            BILL-PAYROLL-USSA.
       IF EMP-PAY-SUCCESSFUL-CALL
           NEXT SENTENCE
       ELSE
           PERFORM 8000-IMS-DB-ERROR THRU 8099-EXIT.
       MOVE CMND-NULL TO EMP-U-CC1
                         PROJ-U-CC1
                         BILL-U-CC1.
   6099-EXIT.
       EXIT.
```

B.   PHYSICAL ORGANIZATION

The same recommendations made for physically organizing
the code of a non-IMS program should be applied to an IMS
program as well. Indentation and spacing should be
utilized to visually enhance the code.

1. IFs

Any IF which tests a status code from a data base call
should immediately follow, and be aligned with, that
call.

2. CALLs

All arguments for a given CALL should be indented and
each should be on a separate line.

3. ENTRY

There can be only one ENTRY statement. Each PCB on
the ENTRY should be indented and placed on a separate
line.

C.   COBOL VERBS - SPECIAL CONSIDERATIONS

Special consideration should be given to the use of some
COBOL verbs under IMS. In the IMS message processing
environment, where time and storage utilization become
critical, those COBOL verbs which are relatively expensive
in terms of these resources should be avoided.

1. ACCEPT

ACCEPT should not be used in any IMS program.

2. CLOSE

Since OS files cannot be accessed in a message
processing program, the CLOSE is not used in those
programs.

3. DISPLAY/EXHIBIT

DISPLAY and EXHIBIT should not be used in a message
processing program.

4. EXAMINE/STRING/TRANSFORM/UNSTRING

These verbs are very time-consuming and, therefore,
very costly. They should be avoided in any program,
but particularly in a message processing program.

5. ON

The ON conditional verb cannot be used in a message processing program because these programs must be serially reusable.

6. OPEN

Open cannot be used in message processing programs since they cannot process OS files.

7. TRACE

Use of the COBOL TRACE option is not advised since the program must be recompiled after debugging to remove the trace statements. BTS is better suited to testing and debugging of IMS programs.

D. EFFICIENCY

The efficiency of an IMS program will be determined to a large degree by the method in which data is accessed and updated. Every IMS program should strive to minimize required processing time by meeting two major objectives.

1. Minimize the number of DL/I calls.

2. Select call parameters which result in the shortest path to the data.

The following techniques should be utilized in order to satisfy the above goals.

1. SEQUENCE OF CALLS

A program processing a data base or data base record sequentially should access the segments in hierarchical sequence. Root segments in HIDAM or HISAM data bases should be read in key-field sequence. Dependent segments should be retrieved by occurrence in key field sequence, and by segment type top-to-bottom and left-to-right. Advantages of sequencing calls in this manner are:

a. Chances are improved that the desired segment will already be in a buffer area as a result of a previous I/O operation. Consequently, no physical I/O will be necessary.

b. Under the HDAM and HIDAM access methods, pointers are generally maintained in the forward direction only. Probability is increased that IMS will require additional I/O if a desired segment is backwards in the data base record.

2. COMMAND CODES

The proper use of command codes in segment search arguments can greatly enhance a program's efficiency. The following paragraphs describe several of the more powerful command codes and their uses.

a. PATH CALL - COMMAND CODE 'D'

Often a program will require data from several segments within a hierarchical path. The program should utilize the path call in order to retrieve or insert all required segments in one hierarchical path as part of a single DL/I call.

b. NO-REPLACE-COMMAND CODE 'N'

When a program has retrieved segments for update using a path call, but does not update all the segments in the path, the NO-REPLACE command code should be used to prevent replacement of those segments which(1) were not changed, or (2) require additional updating after processing other dependent segments (e.g., when creating summary totals of dependent segment fields).

c. ESTABLISH PARENTAGE - COMMAND CODE 'P'

The command code 'P' may be used to request IMS to establish parentage at a segment other than that which would normally result. This command may be effectively used in combination with the path command to establish parentage at the root while also retrieving dependent segments. This eliminates the need to issue a get call specifically for the root and then additional get-next-within-parent for the lower level segments.

d. LAST - COMMAND CODE 'L'

When a program must access a segment which is known to be physically last of multiple occurrences (e.g., segments which are sequenced by date) use the 'L' command to skip preceding occurrences of the segment.

3. USE OF POSITIONING

The multi-positioning option can be used in some circumstances to avoid repeating data base calls to re-establish position within a data base record. Multiple PCBs can frequently be used to maintain position on multiple data base records and save get unique calls which would otherwise be necessary to move back and forth.

XI.
SUBROUTINE
LOGIC — IMS

A.   IMS ERROR ROUTINE

The IMS error routine will be performed when an IMS call
returns an unexpected status code. Parameters used by the
error routine must be set up before it is performed.
These parameters are as follows:

1.   The paragraph name of the errant call.

2.   The function code.

3.   The SSA(s).

4.   The PCB.

```
8000-IMS-DB-ERROR.
     DISPLAY '*****************************************'.
     DISPLAY '*            IMS DB ERROR REPORT        *'.
     DISPLAY '*****************************************'.
     DISPLAY 'ERROR OCCURRED IN PARAGRAPH .' DB-ERR-PARA.
     DISPLAY 'DATA BASE DEFINTION..........' DB-ERR-DBD-NAME.
     DISPLAY 'FUNCTION.....................' DB-ERR-FUNC.
     DISPLAY 'LEVEL........................' DB-ERR-LEVEL.
     DISPLAY 'STATUS.......................' DB-ERR-STATUS.
     DISPLAY 'PROCESSING OPTION............' DB-ERR-PROC-OPT.
     DISPLAY 'LAST SEGMENT ACCESSED........' DB-ERR-LAST-SEG.
     MOVE    DB-ERR-KEY-LEN TO DB-ERR-CONV.
     DISPLAY 'KEY FEEDBACK LENGTH..........' DB-ERR-CONV.
     MOVE    DB-ERR-CNT-SEN-SEG TO DB-ERR-CONV.
     DISPLAY 'NO OF SENSITIVE SEGMENTS.....' DB-ERR-CONV.
     DISPLAY 'KEY FEEDBACK.................' DB-ERR-KEY-FDBK.
     DISPLAY 'SSA.........................' DB-ERR-SSA-1.
     MOVE    LIT-YES                 TO     SW-ERROR-CALL.

8099-EXIT.
     EXIT.
```

NOTE: The above IMS error routine does not cause the
        program to ABEND nor does it stop processing. The
        logic in the program should recognize the error
        condition and exit normally. Other IMS error
        routines (especially in production programs) may be
        designed to force program termination in cases of
        unusual return conditions.

B.   IMS SYMBOLIC CHECKPOINT/RESTART

Batch IMS programs and Batch Message Processing programs
which issue update calls to a data base and have sequential files defined as GSAM data bases should use the
following logic:

```
  0000-DRIVER.
*****
*****     FIRST CALL IS THE RESTART CALL
*****
      PERFORM 8000-RESTART THRU 8099-EXIT.
      IF IO-STATUS-CODE EQUAL STC-SUCCESSFUL-CALL
*****
*****     IF THE RESTART IO AREA IS EQUAL TO SPACES THEN THIS
*****         IS A NORMAL EXECUTION OF THE PROGRAM.  THEREFORE
*****         A CHECKPOINT CALL SHOULD BE ISSUED SO THAT THE
*****         PROGRAM CAN BE BACKED OUT TO THE BEGINNING.
*****
          IF XRST-IO-AREA EQUALS SPACES
              PERFORM 8100-CHECKPOINT THRU 8199-EXIT
*****
*****     OTHERWISE THE PROGRAM IS BEING RESTARTED.
*****         RESTORE THE CHECKPOINT-ID FIELD & REPOSITION
*****         THE ACCOUNT MASTER FILE WITH A GU CALL USING
*****         THE INFORMATION FROM THE SAVE AREA.
*****         AS THE CURRENT TRANSACTION FILE IS A GSAM
*****         DATA BASE IT IS AUTOMATICALLY REPOSITIONED.
*****
          ELSE
              MOVE XRST-ID TO CHECKPOINT-ID
              MOVE AN-OPER-GREATER-EQUAL TO AM-ROOT-Q-OPER
              MOVE SAVE-ACCT-NUMBER TO AM-ROOT-Q-KEYVAL
              PERFORM 8200-GU-ACCT-MAST-ROOT THRU 8299-EXIT
              MOVE AN-OPER-EQUAL TO AM-ROOT-Q-OPER.
*****
*****     IF ALL IMS CALLS SUCCESSFUL PROCESS ACCOUNT MASTER
*****
      IF SW-IMS-CALLS-OK
          PERFORM 1000-PROCESS-ACCOUNT-MASTER THRU 1099-EXIT
              UNTIL SW-END-OF-DB.

  8000-RESTART.
*****
*****     THIS IS THE RESTART CALL WHICH SHOULD BE PERFORMED
*****     ONLY ONCE AS THE FIRST CALL IN THE PROGRAM
*****
      MOVE SPACES TO XRST-IO-AREA.
      CALL "CBLTDLI' USING FUNC-RESTART
                          IO-PCB
                          LNTH-IO-AREA
                          XRST-IO-AREA
                          LTH-SAVE-AREA
                          SAVE-AREA.
      IF NOT IO-SUCCESSFUL-CALL
          MOVE IO-PCB TO IO-ERR-PCB
          MOVE '8000-RESTART' TO IO-ERR-PARA
          MOVE FUNC-RESTART TO IO-ERR-FUNC
          PERFORM 8900-IMS-DC-ERROR THRU 8999-EXIT.
```

```
8099-EXIT.
    EXIT.

8100-CHECKPOINT.
*****
*****     THIS IS THE CHECKPOINT CALL
*****
    CALL 'CBLTDLI' USING FUNC-CHECKPOINT
                         IO-PCB
                         LNTH-IO-AREA
                         CHECKPOINT-ID
                         LTH-SAVE-AREA
                         SAVE-AREA.
    IF NOT IO-SUCCESSFULL-CALL
        MOVE IO-PCB TO IO-ERR-PCB
        MOVE '8010-CHECKPONT' TO IO-ERR-PARA
        MOVE FUNC-CHECKPOINT TO IO-ERR-FUNC
        PERFORM 8900-IMS-DC-ERROR THRU 8999-EXIT.
8199-EXIT.
    EXIT.
```